Show Your Work

Teaching Smarter with the Science of Learning

Beth Hawks

BLOOMSBURY ACADEMIC
NEW YORK • LONDON • OXFORD • NEW DELHI • SYDNEY

BLOOMSBURY ACADEMIC
Bloomsbury Publishing Inc, 1359 Broadway, New York, NY 10018, USA
Bloomsbury Publishing Plc, 50 Bedford Square, London, WC1B 3DP, UK
Bloomsbury Publishing Ireland, 29 Earlsfort Terrace, Dublin 2, D02 AY28, Ireland

First published in the United States of America 2026

For legal purposes the Acknowledgments on pp. viii–ix constitute an extension of this copyright page.

A catalog record for this book is available from the Library of Congress

ISBN: HB: 979-8-2163-7851-8
PB: 979-8-2163-7850-1
ePDF: 979-8-2163-7853-2
eBook: 979-8-2163-7852-5

Typeset by Newgen KnowledgeWorks Pvt. Ltd., Chennai, India

For product safety related questions contact productsafety@bloomsbury.com.

To find out more about our authors and books visit www.bloomsbury.com and sign up for our newsletters.

Show Your Work

For Mr. Sandberg

You could never know how much you mean to me.

Thank you for keeping me curious.

Thank you for supporting me for almost four decades.

Contents

Acknowledgments

This book is only possible because I am surrounded by love and support from

Mom and Dad: I know it was a surprise when I said I felt led to leave my very stable job to try this. Thanks for supporting me, not only with love and prayers but also with peanut butter and frequent flyer miles.

GRACE Christian School: GRACE was my professional home for twenty-one years, but it was more than that. It was a loving community where I laughed, cried, and prayed with my colleagues and administration daily. Thank you for giving me space to grow, allowing me to try new things, and helping me clean up the mess when the new things sometimes fell apart. Thanks for staying in my corner, even after I left.

Blue Pod Plus: All members—current, past, and honorary. We've shared so much, and I love you more than words could say.

Andrew Watson, John Almarode, and Kevin Washburn: I basically found you online and badgered you into being friends with me. I appreciate all the help and support you have given me professionally, but more than that I value the friendship I have with each of you.

Jay, Liz, Stacey, Tom, Julie, and Dana: The YMCA turned my world upside down in the best possible ways. Thanks for showing me what excellent instruction looks like outside the academic setting. You are more than group fitness instructors. You are amazing educators.

Matt: There is a direct line from what takes place in Studio 1 to the writing of this book. You built strength and confidence in me that wasn't there before. Thank you for sharing your heart with everyone you meet, including this clumsy girl with no balance and not enough boundaries. Thank you to both you and Steven for allowing me to treat you like unpaid therapists when I just start spilling my guts without warning.

Every teacher I had: Teaching has always been difficult because it requires the investment of your whole heart. Mrs. Doane, Miss Crowder, Mr. Dorrin, Mr. Watkins, Mr. Freeman, Mr. Sandberg, Mrs. Demby, Mr. Barbara, and many others, thank you for giving your hearts and contributing to the person I am today. I hope you see yourselves in these pages.

Introduction

There are so many education books written by people much smarter and more well-informed than I, so why would I think this one is needed? That is a great question. I read a lot of books on education, cognitive science, and the science of learning, and I will recommend many of them to you. While I love those works and consume them voraciously, most of them are not written by classroom teachers. They are written by researchers or research communicators. That's great because we get to hear directly from those who have done the experimental work, but it may mean they haven't seen how it plays out in an actual classroom. It also means they may lack the perspective of how their advice works out when the eighth-grade girls you just put in a jigsaw group are experiencing social drama or when the kid who wants to entertain creatively uses his whiteboard for anything but the purpose you intended.

Much scientific research is carried out in graduate school labs where participants memorize lists of words or syllables rather than academic content. Occasionally, experiments are carried out in a highly structured classroom experiment in which as many variables are controlled for as possible. That's right and appropriate because that's what science is, but the application of such research is a messier process. Scientific experiments isolate variables; teachers blend them. Unfortunately, little research is currently carried out in "the wild," by which I mean actual classrooms with actual students learning actual curriculum from their actual teacher. You and I know that you cannot control most variables in your classroom. The books I read on the science of learning also tend to be written from a fairly idealistic perspective, as though all students will respond perfectly to the right techniques. That's never been my experience as students arrive in my class with their own desires and opinions, like fully formed humans tend to do.

I wanted to write a book for teachers in which they could imagine their own classrooms as they read, so I will share stories and examples from real science teachers. I wanted to give realistic advice along with all the caveats and complexities. We all know teaching is a complicated process and rarely looks neat and tidy. We shouldn't hide from that; we should embrace and honor it. It's part of what makes the work so interesting. I want reading this book to feel like you and I are sitting in the teachers' lounge, sharing stories and ideas. I hope you will laugh at my foibles and recognize your own. I hope you will recognize your strengths and build on them. I hope, by the end of this book, you will feel empowered and encouraged to continue in the noble work of educating young minds by seeing how research can inform your practice as you teach students. And, I hope you will share techniques with colleagues and explain them to students and parents. The title *Show Your Work* was chosen because I believe we should be explicit about why we do what we do.

Before we start, let me tell you how I got here. My life has been defined by curiosity. According to Harvard Researcher Paul Harris, children ask about forty thousand questions between the ages of two and five, averaging a rate of twenty-five per hour, mostly starting with the word why. Why is the sky blue? Why do cows give milk? Why do flowers smell good but dog poop smells bad? Most kids grow out of that, but I didn't. Every day, I still ask why the things around me work the way that they do.

I owe a lot to a great many teachers, but the one who put up with me the most was Mr. Don Sandberg, my ninth-grade physical science teacher. As you can imagine, I was a demanding learner. I probably asked him 147 questions per week. I wanted to know how a key opened a lock, how the gas pump knew when your tank was full so it could shut itself off, and why the same note played on different musical instruments sounded different. He patiently answered almost every question I asked. I only remember one question that he told me he couldn't answer because I didn't know enough about math yet. At the time, I was convinced I would understand it if he would just try to explain it to me, but when I finally got to introductory calculus, I realized he was right and I would not have understood. Halfway through the year, Mr. Sandberg recommended that I buy the book *The Way Things Work* by David Macaulay, a move I now realize was as much for his sanity as for my curiosity. I used that book a lot, and I still have it. It is sitting next to my desk right now. Before Google, it was my go-to resource. In a casual conversation that I'm certain he doesn't remember, Mr. Sandberg said to me, "This curiosity you have is an important part of you." Because of my adoration and respect for him, that moment was huge. I can't tell you how important it was for a fourteen-year-old nerd girl to hear that; not only was it a good thing to be asking all of these questions, it was an "important part" of who I was. My decision to become a science teacher was due, in no small part, to that conversation. In my senior year of high school, I fell in love with physics because of the energy of my fantastic teacher, Mr. Jim Barbara. I had his class at the end of the day, so I stayed after school frequently to ask him many questions about how things work. His enthusiastic willingness to share knowledge with me propelled me to even deeper questions and ultimately into teaching physics because I wanted to share that love of knowledge with others. The power teachers have is immense.

My teacher training was similar to that of everyone else who went to education school in the mid-nineties. It was mostly about the theories of Maslow, Piaget, and Skinner. It focused heavily on VAK (Visual, Auditory, and Kinetic) "learning styles" and cooperative learning. I had exactly one class on meeting the special needs of children with disabilities, and it covered every scenario, ranging from ADHD to students with feeding tubes. My assessment class was entirely about portfolios because my professors thought grades were clearly coming to an end and portfolios were the "direction education was headed." This is a phrase I have come to loathe as I recognize how fad-driven education is. The only time I remember questioning any of this was when we talked about Skinner boxes, and I asked why we assumed that humans learned in the same way as birds. The professor sort of blew off the question because I'm sure it wasn't the first time a student had asked it. But I figured these were people who knew what they were talking about, so I didn't press it much.

A decade later, I'd been teaching for a while and had a more realistic view of teaching, but I still operated in the world of "learning styles" and discovery. At a professional development conference, I attended a session on what was then called brain-based learning. I found it exciting and interesting, but I didn't find a lot of resources that seemed like anything other than sales pitches. Because of that, other than a few techniques I picked up at the conference, it slipped into the background of my mind.

Then, Cheryl Herrington, the math teacher next door to me, recommended a book called *The Brain That Changes Itself* by Norman Doidge, MD. Around the same time I discovered a writer named Kevin Washburn and his book *The Architecture of Learning*. Doidge's book is a fascinating study of neuroplasticity, which opposed what I had been taught while I was growing up about our brains being pretty much fixed after age ten. This was a concept I had always found strange because the people who told it to me were middle school teachers, who I assumed were trying to change my brain after the age of ten. I was also suspicious of this idea as an adult because I had taught a girl who underwent a hemispherectomy. She had the entire left half of her brain removed to treat Rasmussen's Syndrome, and she had relearned how to speak and read at the age of fourteen. Kevin Washburn's book is about constructing a lesson based on how the brain processes new information and has been a valuable resource when planning especially complex topics. Reading these two books back to back revolutionized the way I viewed my students and my lessons. While it is weird for me to consider this now, that summer was the first time I recognized that neurological and psychological research could provide insight into how I teach. I had not considered that the people who study brains could help me make better use of the brain for teaching students. That summer was the start of a slow walk down the path of studying cognitive science and education, but I was seeking out things on my own and didn't know how to separate what was valuable from what was merely trendy. Seeking out valuable cognitive science research can be a challenge. As Edward Watson and Bradley Busch acknowledge in the introduction to their book *The Science of Learning: 99 Studies That Every Teacher Needs to Know*, "the wealth of research out there was stuck behind paywalls, difficult to locate, and not obviously translatable into practical strategies."

That all changed in 2018, the year I attended my first Learning and the Brain conference. A brochure landed in my school mailbox, and while I was on my way to the recycling bin with it, a speaker caught my attention. By the end of my morning door duty, I was ready to pack my bags. I begged my administrators to send me to this conference, and they agreed as long as I would do a presentation about what I had learned upon returning home. My academic world was turned upside down at that conference. I couldn't believe how much research there was and how kind the presenters were to people like me with dozens of questions (I told you). It was like I had found "my people" in the world of education. Since I didn't want to ask the school to pay for it again, I asked my parents if they could send me the following year as a birthday gift, and they agreed. That was the year I became hooked for life. I found the keynote speeches of Barbara Oakley, Sarah Jayne Blakemore, David Daniel, and David Rose fascinating. I discovered Andrew Watson's writing on working memory and attention. I met and developed a professional crush on John Almarode. In the years since, I have gotten to connect with Daniel

Willingham both online and in person and have discovered the podcasts of Craig Barton. I have connected with many other educational heroes online, even some in the UK. The world of cognitive science in education is a great source of information that can benefit teachers at all levels, and the Learning and the Brain conference was my introduction to that world.

Once you see how the knowledge of cognitive science works in teaching, you can't unsee it; so I started requesting additional time in faculty meetings to present to my colleagues, and we are all better teachers as a result. We do many of the same things we used to as a matter of intuition and experience, but now we approach our practices more intentionally and confidently, knowing how and why they work. Throughout the time of virtual learning during the COVID-19 pandemic, I was grateful I had spent time learning about how students learn because it allowed me to focus on what mattered, regardless of venue, and to have some degree of confidence in making decisions about things I had never encountered before.

Now, we arrive at the writing of this book. I want all teachers to get the benefit I have gotten from studying these concepts. I want you to think about how discoveries made in the lab might look in your classroom, recognizing the differences between those contexts, so you can adapt their conclusions and methods to yours. As Andrew Watson says in every presentation, "Don't do this thing. Think this way." Researchers can't and shouldn't make decisions for your classroom, but their work can inform the decisions you make. While I am focusing on the science classroom because that is the context that I know best, I hope those of you who teach math, history, art, literature, theater, technology, or foreign languages will see yourselves in these pages as well and use your professional judgment to translate the ideas you find here into your content.

I'll start each chapter with a story. Some are from my own classroom or that of a colleague; others are from my group fitness classes at the YMCA or memories from my childhood. After all, teaching and learning happen everywhere. I'm going to mention my classes at the YMCA pretty frequently for two reasons. First, taking classes there has given me a chance to observe educational techniques in another setting, and I want to acknowledge the fine group of educators I have met there. The other reason is that I became a novice learner for the first time in decades when I started taking group fitness classes in 2023, and experiencing that feeling again gave me greater empathy for my students. After telling a story, I'll share some of the relevant research on each topic and provide you with some great resources so you can dig deeper if you want to. I'll end each chapter with how this can look in all of our classrooms and stories from our colleagues.

There are dozens of topics that could be covered in a book like this, but it would be overwhelming to include them all. This is a top-ten list of ideas that had the most impact in my classroom and those around me. There is a lot of overlap between topics, so if it starts to feel repetitive, it is because of how each topic relates to those before. We will start with working memory because you will save yourself and your students a lot of frustration if you design your lessons with working memory in mind. We will end with formative assessment because it ties the rest of the topics together so well.

- Working Memory—Learning about working memory changed my approach to lesson design more than any other concept in recent years. As I read the research, I had a few "aha" moments, recognizing times when my lessons had been unsuccessful because of the overload I had put on my students, deluding myself into thinking I was helping them think better by "increasing rigor." I now approach my lessons with more of a "Price is Right" mindset, asking myself "How can I get them right to their limit without going over?"
- Clarity—Since we can't implement all the good things we find in research books, I always do a cost–benefit analysis before applying what I've learned. How high is the impact of this practice? How much time and energy will be invested in implementing it? If the impact is low, I will only attempt it if the time cost is also low. If the impact is high, I am willing to spend more time implementing it. If the time cost is very high, the impact must be very high to make it worth the effort. In the case of clarity, I find the best of both worlds. It is the ideal balance of being highly effective while requiring little time to make it part of a classroom routine.
- Prior Knowledge and Schema—It is likely that you already activate prior knowledge in your lessons. Most teachers do this as a matter of intuition. The reason I included it in this book is that understanding how schema is constructed made me more intentional about how I connected new knowledge to students' existing knowledge. Adding informed intentionality to your intuition makes this practice even more powerful.
- Focus and Diffuse Modes—The first time I heard Barbara Oakley explain the two modes of our thinking, it was like a light turned on in

my brain. We've all had the experience of getting caught in a thinking loop only to think of the right answer in the car on the way home, and we have had students trapped there too. Learning about focused and diffuse modes gave me ways to advise students about how they can get out of that frustrating cycle.

- Rich Encoding Using Metaphors, Demos, Labs, and Connections—Science teachers are well-versed in the use of demonstrations and labs, but we can use them more effectively with some reflection. One of the things my students have often told me they like about my teaching is the use of metaphors and the way I break down terms to connect with other disciplines, so I was thrilled to find that there is good research backing for their use.
- The Dangers of Discovery Learning and Hyperfocusing on Engagement—Labs and projects are good, and they can be inspiring to students if we use them well. If we use them as "discovery learning" with minimal guidance, however, they can be frustrating experiences for students and result in little learning. We, as a profession, have become hyperfocused on engagement, and nothing looks more engaging than a project or a lab in which students are doing everything. Student engagement is a necessary means to the end of learning, not the end itself. The research is clear that giving students minimal guidance does not ultimately result in more learning, especially for those with fewer experiences from which to build schema, so I'll make a case for high-quality, interactive direct instruction with lab experiences and projects that come after concepts have been encoded. You can look forward to my story of failure when attempting to conduct a challenge-based learning project for the first time.
- Modeling and Scaffolding—I think I model well, but scaffolding is a tricky concept for me, and I'm not sure I always implement it well. I think that can probably be said of many teachers. I included it here because I wanted to learn more about it from the research and because I wanted to ask my colleagues about it so I could learn from them. Passing it on to you is a bonus.
- When to Memorize—I have sat in more than one professional development seminar in which I was told that students should not be required to memorize anything they can Google. There are

videos online that imply or outright state that we now live in a world where knowledge is no longer necessary and demand a revolution in education that will only focus on "twenty-first century skills," not knowledge. Yet every teacher knows that there is a limit to what students can do with knowledge they have just looked up. Some information is only useful when it is firmly in their heads. My hope is that this chapter will give you a way to decide what knowledge your students actually need to have stored in their long-term memory and not to shy away from insisting that they do.

- Retrieval Practice—When I first learned about retrieval practice, I wondered what all the hoopla was about. I thought it was no big deal. After all, haven't we all been asking students review questions forever? Then I read *Powerful Teaching* by Pooja Agarwal and Patrice Bain, and it was clear to me that I had not been taking full advantage of this high-impact teaching tool. When I started finding ways to work retrieval practice into my daily routine rather than only in review sessions, my students' performance and learning improved dramatically.
- Formative Assessment—As you might imagine in a practice as complex as teaching, there is a fair amount of overlap between many of these topics. I'll end with formative assessment because it wraps up the rest of the topics well. Formative assessment is often done via retrieval practice and gives students more clarity. Retrieval practice is frequently about memorized knowledge or activating what they already know. And all of this may be used to help build schema by encoding new content and off-load working memory. None of our practices occur in a vacuum. Mostly, formative assessments help us teach more effectively because they give us insight into the minds of our students as they learn so that we can adjust our teaching at that moment rather than after a test reveals their lack of understanding.

In writing this book, I knew I needed examples from multiple levels of teaching, so I needed to interview great teachers. I happen to have easy access to the best ones there are because I work with them or have worked with them in the past. Since you are going to be reading their names a lot, allow me to introduce you.

- Melanie Dunning—Melanie currently teaches honors chemistry, AP chemistry, physics, and engineering, but she has also had experience with elementary and middle school STEM courses and all forms of upper school science. She earned a BS in secondary science education and BA in chemistry from NC State University. What you most need to know about Melanie is that she is a proud science nerd, and she and her students adore each other.

- Hannah Eichhorst—Hannah was my student for two years in high school. I taught her chemistry and physics. After getting her BS in geology, she returned to my school to teach middle and high school earth science and AP environmental science, and it was a joy to have her as a colleague. After earning her MA in teaching middle grades education, she began leading a team of seventh-grade science teachers. What you most need to know about Hannah is that she truly enjoys and believes in middle schoolers.
- Alyssa Powell—Alyssa has a BS in nutrition and dietetics from the Ohio State University and a masters in secondary science education—life sciences from Xavier. Her specialty is teaching biology and anatomy, but she also has experience with seventh-grade earth science, high school earth science, and AP environmental science, which are the classes she currently teaches. What you most need to know about Alyssa is that she believes kids will rise to whatever level of challenge she gives them, so she sets high standards and supports them in reaching those standards.
- Cassidy Scholten—Cassidy has a BA in elementary education. She teaches science to little people in third and fourth grade as well as introducing sixth-grade students to the world of middle school science. What you most need to know about Cassidy is that she works hard to prepare her students for future science learning by showing them both the wonder and the rigor of lab sciences before they are too jaded to resist putting in the work.
- Zane Smitley—Zane entered the teaching profession as a middle school history teacher, but he had a background as a chiropractor and offered to create a high school anatomy course from scratch. A few years later, when the school wanted to expand their advanced placement offerings, he volunteered to take on AP biology. Eventually, he stopped teaching history and added freshman biology to his repertoire and has been teaching life sciences for over a decade. I know his teaching well as our classrooms were not more than two

doors away from each other for twenty-one years, and I can often hear him teaching through our adjoining wall. What you most need to know about Zane is that he believes students who challenge themselves will find the confidence to grow even more, and he has inspired many of our students to pursue degrees in biology and careers in medicine.

Now that we know where we are going and who our fellow teachers are, I hope you will do more than read this book. I hope you will pause occasionally and put the book down to think about your own classroom, both the mountain top moments and the dismal valleys. Think about the things you have done that worked well and those that didn't. Use a notepad to reflect on why a lesson was successful and how you can strengthen it even further. If a lesson was unsuccessful, pause to think about where it went wrong and whether it is worth redesigning with research-backed techniques or throwing it out altogether. Combine the lessons learned from those experiences with the stories of the science teachers and students I interviewed here and the good research being done by scientists to make each year more effective than the one before. I hope you will feel challenged to improve, but I also hope you feel encouraged that you are doing good work now. What I most hope is that this book increases your confidence in decision-making and makes you feel secure that the things you do are beneficial for you and your students.

1 Working Memory

It was the start of a physics class, and I wanted to do a little retrieval practice to connect yesterday's lesson to today's. This is common, and my students are used to it. They know the rules are that they have to give me a guess, and I won't move on if they say, "I don't know." They must give me some kind of attempt. This day, it went a little pear-shaped.

> **Me:** "Julia, what is the weakest field force?"
> **Julia:** "I don't know."
> **Me:** "You know I'm not going to accept that. Just guess."
> Long pause
> **Julia:** "I really don't know."
> **Me (not giving up):** "Remember there were four field forces. Just tell me one of them. It's okay if you're wrong."
> **Julia (in complete catastrophic freeze):** Stares blankly at me for a long time followed by "I just don't know."
> I finally gave up and told her the answer was gravity just so we could move on.

Later that night, I got a very kind email from her very patient mom.

> Julia doesn't know I'm writing to you, but I want to explain what happened today. She couldn't remember the word in English. Then, she couldn't remember any words in English other than "I don't know." I told her that you love her and were just trying to do what was best for her, but I wanted you to know that she wasn't just trying to get out of answering the question.

Julia is adopted from another country and had only lived in America for four years, but her English was so good that I sometimes forgot it was her second language and that she was still likely translating things in her head before she said them. I was horrified that I had not taken that into account and grateful for her mother's gracious response. I apologized and thanked her and told her I would absolutely handle it differently in the future. I was able to talk to Julia and repair the damage, and we ended the year with a great relationship, but it could have easily gone the other way because I didn't consider that I was taxing her working memory beyond its limit.

When I engage my students in retrieval practice, I usually have everyone answer on mini-whiteboards, but I sometimes use popsicle sticks with students' names on them to call on students individually. When I do, I try to ask each student a question I believe they can answer with a little thought or support because it is never my goal to embarrass anyone. Because these questions are meant as a warm-up at the beginning of class or cooldown at the end, I keep the questions pretty simple. The reason I won't allow them to say, "I don't know" and move on is that, as soon as I allow that, every student will say they don't know. It will become synonymous with "leave me alone." This is a good policy, and I stand by it, but the experience I had with Julia changed the way I address a student not knowing, and thanks to an episode of Craig Barton's Podcast "Tips for Teachers," in which Dylan William shares ways to keep "don't know" from being the end of the conversation, I now have techniques that I can use to prevent this from happening again. I'll discuss them later in this chapter.

The management of working memory may be one of the trickiest and most important things we do in the classroom. Once a student has reached the limit of their working memory, we aren't going to get much out of them. In his book *Learning Begins*, Andrew Watson compares it to an attempt to sort photos for a themed album on a table that is too small for the task. If you try to put more photos on the table than it can hold, they will start falling off, and you will not be able to combine them into anything meaningful. In the same way, every teacher has experienced a moment when the information they were trying to teach started "falling off the table" of their students' minds, and they were no longer able to do anything meaningful with it.

Human brains can only hold a few things in active use at any given moment. According to Nelson Cowan's 2001 article on the Cambridge University Press website, for most of us, the limit is about four when it comes to things we can analyze in detail. When that limit is reached, using other sources will not help, making it important to avoid reaching that point.

Researchers have spent decades trying to find out if there are ways to increase our working memory capacity. So far, they have come up empty. Working memory, it seems, is a relatively fixed quantity, increasing from childhood to its peak in your early twenties and then decreasing ever so slightly afterward. While that seems like terrible news, it's not a bug; it's a feature of our design. If we tried to process too many things at once without limit, we would have trouble making simple decisions. If you will excuse a nerd moment, an episode of *Star Trek Voyager* springs to mind. In it, Seven of Nine, the former Borg rescued by Captain Janeway, downloads the ship's computer into her own brain. Her behavior becomes strange as she treats everyone with suspicion, eventually spinning out multiple contradictory conspiracy theories about every member of the crew. At the end of the episode, The Doctor reaches the conclusion that her human brain was trying to process too much information at once and could not interpret it properly. Our limited working memory is a gift. Without it, we might, like Seven of Nine, try to relate too many things to each other at once and reach very wrong conclusions. This limitation can, however, pose a problem if not handled properly by educators. We have to recognize that far-off look in a student's eyes that shows there is no more room for processing.

Fortunately, we have more than our limited working memory to aid us as we think. We also have long-term memory, and it can engage in the heavy lifting we need for truly complex learning. A fact that is stored in long-term memory doesn't take up as much space in our working memory, so having a lot of interconnected facts enables us to use our limited working memory for the harder work. In a 2023 Learning and the Brain conference session, Jim Heal of Deans for Impact called the interaction between long-term memory and working memory "a merry dance." Things are pulled from long-term memory into working memory, enhancing how the new learning is then stored. This back and forth between working memory and long-term memory is at the heart of what we do with our students.

In his book *How to Explain Absolutely Anything to Absolutely Anyone*, Andy Tharby discusses how items stored in long-term memory can be brought back into the working memory space when needed. "If a child knows their times tables," he says, "they can use this knowledge to solve more complex problems without placing any extra stress on the working memory." This is also true of element symbols, names of muscles, Newton's laws of motion, and the definition of sedimentary. If we want students to engage in higher-level thinking, there are some things that must be stored in long-term memory first. I am not suggesting that students should memorize everything, so we will address how to make that decision in Chapter 8. What I am suggesting is that we cannot have kids memorize little or nothing just because "they can Google it."

We can use mnemonic devices to aid our working memory because they combine multiple pieces of information into a word or short sentence. Since focusing on meaning will help information transfer into long-term memory more effectively, Daniel Willingham, in his book *Outsmart Your Brain*, advises that we only use mnemonic devices where there is no obvious meaning that would be helpful, like memorizing the order of the waves of the electromagnetic spectrum or the names of the bones in the wrist. Having students create their own mnemonic devices might be even more helpful as the very act of creating it would require them to think about meaning. In his classic book *Why Don't Students Like School*, Willingham gives a variety of other methods for aiding memorization, like setting content to music and chants or drawing a picture, both methods that require focus on meaning.

In their article entitled "Cognitive-Load Theory: Methods to Manage Working Memory Load in the Learning of Complex Tasks," Fred Paas and Jeroen J. G. Van Merriënboer state, "To acquire new knowledge, learners have to allocate working memory (WM) capacity to—that is, invest mental effort in—learning tasks. In the ideal situation, WM resources required for learning do not exceed the available resources, and all available resources can be allocated to activities that contribute to the learning process. However, in reality, there will often be high cognitive load." Agreed. It would be lovely if students came to our classrooms with no extraneous items in their working memories and there were no distractions from the environment, but that is just not the universe we live in. We can't remove their internal monologues, their worries about other classes, or their nervous anticipation of this afternoon's play audition. We have little control over sounds coming from the hallway or air conditioner repair men walking on the roof above our classrooms. Heaven forbid a bug comes into your room; I'm convinced those take up all four spaces in a student's working memory. We have to put our energy into those things over which we have control. We can and should design lessons that maximize their available working memory capacity. As Paas and Van Merriënboer conclude, "Learning tasks should be designed in such a way that the available WM capacity is efficiently used to achieve the highest return on mental effort investment. This means that extraneous load should be minimized so that WM capacity is freed." That means we should not be including extra distractions that do not pertain to the task at hand, like images for their own sake or references to pop culture during difficult parts of the learning.

Managing working memory starts before class. It is much easier to prevent overload than it is to deal with it. Developing routines for your classroom helps to reduce working memory demands because the steps of a process become automated. My students know that the first thing they should do when entering the classroom is to look at the board for the bellwork. I'm not saying they all do it every day without prompting, but most of them do. If there is a routine for entering the lab and beginning the setup, it saves time for giving specific instructions and keeps space free in the working memory for the task of actually performing the experiment. Harry and Rosemary Wong's classic book *The First Days of School* is filled with recommendations for procedures because, even before there was research on how routines help, teachers knew kids got in a lot less trouble if they knew what to do most of the time. Having routines firmly in a student's long-term memory will allow them to remain focused on the germane load rather than wondering what they should do because their pencil is broken. When Peps Mccrea addressed the power of routines in his email newsletter *Evidence Snacks*, he said, "Effective routines set students up for success, free up the precious mental capacity needed for creativity to flourish, and act as a collective ritual which can foster belonging—a key ingredient in meaningful education."

I remember experiencing this phenomenon as a teacher in the early days of the 2020–1 school year, when I was teaching under a hybrid model, teaching both the students in front of me and on a screen. From the moment I walked in the door, the temperature scanners, plexiglass dividers, masks, and iPads drew my attention to how strange my "normal" day had become. Getting the computer and projector set up in such a way that students joining us from home could see what I was doing just as well as the students in front me was a multistep process, involving turning on one microphone and speaker while muting the others, using the projector as a secondary "monitor" visible to those in the room and sharing that screen with the students at home. In the first few weeks, I felt like I had reached working memory overload before the students arrived in my classroom. This process became smoother as it became an automated routine, freeing my mental resources for the other things on which I needed to focus. The same is true of the many routines you develop in your classroom. At first, those seem like too much. They may even seem like they are adding to working memory challenges, but routines reduce the load in the long run—once they become automated. Don't try it once and quit, thinking it didn't work. Again, Peps Mccrea puts it well. His take is that "routines are valuable, but only once they have become automated. Until then, we must treat them as an investment." Be patient, knowing it takes time and repetition for a routine to reach the tipping point where it has become more valuable than difficult. Don't give up on a routine until you have given it a fair shake.

The environment of your classroom also has the potential to impact working memory load. Sit in a student desk and look at your classroom. Would you be distracted by the many forms of sensory input? Are there too many diverting items in their eyeline? I know that is often true in my room. I love my decorations, and it is important to me to share my passion for space exploration, national parks, blood donation, and art with my students so they will see teachers as three-dimensional humans and not curriculum delivery machines.

When I first read the studies on how displays distract students, I didn't want it to be true for *my* classroom. I tried to talk myself into keeping my precious displays by telling myself that the study was done with kindergarten students, and my high school students would not be as distracted. You know that isn't true, and so do I, but if you need proof, similar studies have been repeated with students at all age levels. I thought perhaps, since I leave the same stuff up all year, they would stop being distracted, but three months into the year, a student said, "Whoa! There is a deer in this picture!" I guess he hadn't grown numb to it over time. While I can't bring myself to give them up completely, I have reduced the number of items and thought more about their location. I have started moving the particularly stimulating items to the back and sides of the room. Consider whether you can achieve the same goals with fewer items. I can put up a few large pictures of national parks rather than a lot of small ones. I can choose the highest quality items representing the Apollo era rather than all of the posters, patches, pictures, and stickers that I have collected over the years.

While lesson planning, ask yourself where you might anticipate working memory issues. Look first at the complexity of the skill you are teaching. Is any part of it unnecessarily complicated? If so, simplify it to exactly the things that are needed to accomplish the purpose. I'm not suggesting that you make the class less rigorous but that you eliminate the extraneous details. In my middle school physical science class, I teach about the arrangement of electrons in energy levels, but I intentionally leave out the more complex things they will learn in high school chemistry. There is no need to tell them about d-orbitals and elements that are exceptions to the rule. I know I am not going to ask them to draw a Bohr model for anything larger than argon, so I let them get good at the smaller ones; their high school chemistry teacher will deal with the next level when they are ready for it. I do want them to understand that there will be more, so I say, "We are going to do the simplest ones. It does get more complicated than this in high school, but for now, I just want you to understand the basics." If a student asks about the next level, I give them a quick answer and tell them to stay after class if they are interested in more detail because, while they may be ready, the rest of the class will only be overwhelmed by the influence of quantum mechanics on the atom model. I try to identify these points while I am making the lesson plan.

The biology teacher next door to me, Zane Smitley, told me he gives his lesson a final pass on the morning he is going to teach it. This is a good idea because lesson plans are made several days to a week ahead of time, and things may not have gone as expected between the planning of the lesson and the teaching of it. If there was a fire drill the day before, they may not have the knowledge you expected they would when you designed the plan. They may not have understood the prerequisite information in the previous lessons as much as you thought they would. While brushing your teeth or driving to school, it is a good idea to mentally revisit the lesson plan for the day and adjust. Do some things need to be divided or moved around to reduce working memory demands? How did things go during first period? You might find you need to make a quick adjustment to the plan before you teach the next group of students. Keeping your eyes open to potential working memory load will help you refine your lessons from year to year but also hour to hour.

One of the best things you can do to help with working memory challenges is to identify the purpose of the lesson and stick as much as possible to those things. I'm not saying this is easy. As you can tell from my writing, I tend to get sidetracked with additional details. I want students to understand the awesome nature of the world. There is definitely a place for showing them more than the basics of your curriculum, but if you know a lesson is going to be cognitively demanding, discipline yourself to remove the extras from the flow of your lesson wherever possible. They might get more out of the "extras" if you wait until students have the basics down and then say, "You know what's cool about this?" at the end of the lesson. Hannah Eichhorst, a seventh-grade science teacher, wants her students to be inspired by scientists, but she knows it would be too much for their working memories to process if she talks about the lives of scientists alongside the regular lesson, so she includes a short activity on Mondays that is separate from the content itself, calling it "Mad Scientist Mondays." Keeping them separated means they don't have to hold information about the life of James Hutton in their working memory while also figuring out the features of sedimentary rocks.

Even the way we present information can tax or benefit working memory. As science teachers, we provide a lot of diagrams and labeled images to our students. In a study published in *British Journal of Educational Psychology*, Paul Chandler and John Sweller studied the difference between integrated diagrams (ones in which labels were printed directly on the image) and conventional diagrams (those with the information below or next to the image). Those who were given integrated diagrams were more efficient at processing the information presented as they did not have to switch their attention back and forth between the image and the words. They could take in both simultaneously. They were also able to remember the information better, performing an average of 22 percent better on the subsequent test. Some images are too intricate to directly label, particularly those used in anatomy and biology, but keep it in mind when creating or searching for images. Ask yourself how you can prevent students from having to split their attention and take advantage of the resources that honor that as much as possible.

A year ago, I found a study, referenced in Tharby's book, called "Managing Split-Attention and Redundancy in Multimedia Instruction." It had never occurred to me before that I might be competing with myself for student attention by presenting them with the same information in multiple formats simultaneously. Australian researchers, Slava Kalyuga, Paul Chandler, and John Sweller used computer-based teaching that included both diagrams and texts. In one experiment, they presented the words in auditory-only form, visual-only form, and simultaneous auditory and visual form. According to their article, having both words on the screen and read aloud simultaneously was least effective for learning. The reason was that the two input pathways were carrying verbal information simultaneously. Rather than enhance each other, they competed with each other. As they said, "The visual form was redundant and imposed a cognitive load that interfered with learning." We should not read something to students out loud at the same time we are expecting them to read it. Since then, I have presented the information verbally first, saying, for example, the first law of thermodynamics before projecting it on the board for them to see. Then, I attempt to remain quiet while they read it.

While designing a lesson, figure out where a temporary scaffold might be helpful in reducing working memory load. I'll address scaffolding in more detail in Chapter 7, but it can be really helpful in reducing working memory demands during the early part of learning a complex skill. You might be a teacher who wants students to memorize physics equations. That's fine, but perhaps providing them with a reference list would be useful in the first few days of the chapter, removing it after the point you expect them to have it memorized. It is only fair to let them know when the scaffold will be removed or to make the schedule for its removal a regular part of your routine.

A scaffold doesn't have to be a reference chart or list. The biology teacher Zane Smitley teaches the first link in a chain of processes, like photosynthesis or the sodium-potassium pump, and then asks retrieval questions. Then he teaches the next step and does retrieval with both. He keeps adding to the retrieval questions list as they accumulate knowledge on each new step of the process he's teaching. By the end, the first step should be firmly in their long-term memory, reducing its demand on their working memory as they add the next step. The earth science teacher Alyssa Powell scaffolds to aid working memory simply by planning how to divide the material. If there is a complex topic with related parts, she teaches the parts on separate days or during separate parts of the period before expecting them to put all of the parts into a complete sequence.

If the similarity of two concepts can make it difficult for students to keep them mentally separated, perhaps provide a mnemonic device or keyword on the board. Molarity and molality, for example, have only one letter difference in their name and only a few words of difference in their definitions, yet it is important for chemistry students to distinguish between them if you expect them to do stoichiometry in solutions. Consider reducing the cognitive load just a bit by putting their definitions at the top of the problem set. Scaffolds are never meant to be permanent, but using them until students have committed an idea to long-term memory can be useful in teaching the skill that relies on those basic facts. And, of course, as I mentioned earlier, long-term memory is our best tool for preventing working memory issues.

Another thing to consider when lesson planning is whether you are teaching two new things at the same time. Perhaps you want students to present their learning in the form of a video, Padlet, or digital comic strip. I know when my school began its one-to-one laptop program, it was important for us to expose students to new tools as we didn't want them to always fall back to their comfort zones. This is not much of an issue for us now as our students have been using computers in their learning for their entire school experience and have a wide array of tools with which they are familiar. But, initially, we overloaded them because we were trying to teach new content and new tools at the same time. While trying to categorize different types of energy, they were also required to navigate the Padlet platform for the first time. All of that might have been okay if I hadn't been trying to keep a normal pace at the same time. One of the best pieces of advice in Andrew Watson's *Learning Begins* is to teach new tools with familiar content or new content with familiar tools. I now keep that in mind as I design lessons at the beginning of the year. If there is a platform I know I will want them to use frequently during the year, I make the first assignment in which they use the tool something simple with review material, and keep it very low stakes. The focus is on completing the assignment with the tool, not on the content itself. Later on, when the material is more difficult, they aren't using the tool for the first time. I have also reduced the number of tools I expect them to use, paring down to one or two presentation tools, one organizing tool that is familiar to everyone, and one or two digital retrieval practice tools.

Linking related pieces of information, a process known as chunking, also aids our working memory because a "chunk" may only occupy one space in our working memory even if it contains many parts. This is not true at the beginning of a concept, of course. It comes after the relationship between various items is understood and can be seen as one thing. In a book by Barbara Oakley, T. J. Sejnowski, and A. McConville, *Learning How to Learn*, working memory is represented by a four-armed octopus and is shown trying to juggle the four items it can hold. Each item looks like one metal loop. A few pages later, the octopus is seen holding four chains, each made up of multiple loops. Having a chain made of related concepts allows the working memory to deal with more things simultaneously.

In physical science, when first learning gravitational potential energy and elastic potential energy, there are a lot of obvious differences. Once we see, however, that they are all about storing energy by moving them away from a rest position, they can be seen as one thing that expresses itself in different ways. The same is true of nuclear potential and chemical potential. In the beginning, it is important that students recognize the difference between them, but eventually, you can draw out that these are both cases where energy is stored due to the composition of the matter. UNC professor and president of the International Teaching Learning Cooperative, Dr. Todd Zakrajsek, advises looking for patterns in the material you are learning because "the easier it is to see information as a cluster … the easier it will be to process." He gives the same advice for pattern recognition when reading a textbook that Barbara Oakley advocates, something she calls "a picture walk," which involves skimming the section for bold words, headings, and picture captions before reading a text to give your working memory some hooks to hang the new information on.

I have personally experienced this in the nonacademic learning setting of YMCA cycle classes. In the first class I took, the instructor rapidly went through the various aspects of proper riding form. In less than two seconds, she said, "Head up. Shoulders down. Back straight. Abs lightly braced. Hands light on the handlebars. Elbows soft. Hips back in the saddle. Legs moving in a smooth circular motion. Feet flat." By the time we reached instructions about the lower half of the body, my shoulders were back up next to my ears. It was just too much to take in at once because I did not have enough experience to chunk all of these instructions, making those nine different items that I was trying to hold in my working memory. In my second class, the instructor addressed upper body during the warm-up song and lower body during the first recovery, which was helpful to processing. I don't know if she knows about working memory or if she just naturally divided them, but it was beneficial to me to have her chunk them that way. A few weeks later, I was picturing them as two items because I could visualize head, neck, shoulders, and abs as the shape my upper body should make and picture the hips, legs, knees, and feet as lower body. Now that I have been at it for over two years, it is firmly in long-term memory, providing no load at all. If the instructor cues any part of cycling form, my entire body adapts simultaneously to occupy the correct positions, but this took time, experience, and practice. It wouldn't have happened on the first day.

Depending on the age and experience level of your students, you might engage in the process of chunking differently. With young learners, novice learners, or those with significant learning challenges, you might engage in the process yourself before class and give them the results already chunked. If you teach middle school students, it may be beneficial to model the process in front of them for complex material and then encourage them to do it for themselves on smaller assignments. With high school seniors, it may be appropriate to expect them to do it on their own, especially if you know they have done it before. Consider using a visual image of the chunked information. A poster with a person in proper cycling form would be very useful in the cycle studio, and a poster with the layers of the atmosphere would probably be helpful in an earth science classroom. This would be even more true in a class of students with reading difficulties, auditory processing issues, or English language learners. There are many "right ways" chunk, so give some thought to what will work best with your students.

The use of consistent symbolic hand movements can be an aid to working memory. Physics teachers have long used the right hand rules to represent the relationships between magnetic fields, physical force, and electrical current; and it is always amusing to watch students take that test while twisting their right arm to align with information presented in a problem. Chemistry teacher Melanie Dunning always makes a T (for table) with her hands when saying the words "molar mass" and has her students make a T as well. This is a symbolic reminder to use the periodic table to calculate the molar mass of all compounds. While these are simple gestures that can be done in their seats, motions can be as complex as you choose in order to pair movement with content. When I observed Alyssa Powell's seventh-grade class learning about clouds, she had them stand up with their hands on their heads. She asked them what happened when the pressure was high, and they pushed down on their heads and sank down to show that high pressure causes air to descend. They lifted their hands off of their heads to represent low pressure and wiggled their fingers to show that this causes rain. They had clearly done this multiple times before that day because when she said, "Stand up," they immediately put their hands over their heads. That consistent use of motion had aided, not only their understanding of air masses, but also allowed some of the things they needed to remember to be stored as motions rather than words. When I asked Zane Smitley how much he used gesturing in his teaching to help with working memory demands, his answer was "all of the time." He gave too many examples to list, but something as simple as putting his hands up high and sliding them down low (and having his students do the same) helps them remember the osmotic movement of solutes when there is a concentration gradient.

We've all had some experience with this in multiple contexts outside of the classroom. I can't hear Neil Sadaka's song "Breaking Up is Hard to Do" without going through the arm movements from *Sweatin' to the Oldies 2* in spite of the fact that the last time I did that routine was when I still used VHS tapes. At a summer camp I volunteer for, all of our songs have motions that are related to American Sign Language, and it keeps the kids, aged six through twelve, actively engaged while giving them a way to express and remember the song lyrics. Steve Waltien, a writer of *The Late Show with Stephen Colbert* and actor in the movie *Don't Think Twice*, was interviewed by the *Chicago Tribune* in which he said,

> Spatial things help. That's why as an actor, blocking (the location of the actors onstage during a scene) becomes your friend, because oftentimes it's very easy to memorize something when you can say, "This is the line that I say when I'm standing here, facing out this way; then I turn, put this prop on the table and say this other line." The memory becomes associated with an action.

Think about what gestures or hand motions you might employ as it relates to your own content. It may be as simple as pointing. Zane Smitley teaches anatomy, and having students point to the bone or muscle he is referring to at any given moment helps them reduce their working memory load because their hand is holding the information "in place" rather than having to hold the location in their mind. Asking students to hold up their fingers to represent how many valence electrons are in the elements of each representative family on the periodic table may help them remember it when the time comes to use that information in formula writing. Earth science teachers instinctively represent fault line interactions, such as strike-slip, dip, reverse, and oblique faults with their hands, and they should have students do it too so they can pair a verbal definition with the physical memory of how their hands interacted with each other. Judicious use of gestures can be powerful, so plan them carefully.

Teachers can use their own gestures to accentuate a word or phrase as more important, drawing attention or to represent meaning. In a randomized trial, forty-five college students watched lessons presented by a video. Half of the students watched a lesson that was delivered with speech only, while the other half watched a video that included both speech and gesture. They were then asked to write everything they could remember about the video. Those watching the gesture-enhanced lecture were 33 percent more likely to remember the points that were accompanied by movement. Whether delivering information face-to-face or virtually, it is important that students are able to see the teacher's hands and that the teacher is doing something meaningful with them. There is much research still to be done on the effective use of teacher and student gestures, but if you find something that works, use it.

Planning in anticipation of working memory issues will save you and your students a lot of headaches. Of course, no matter how well we plan, there will be working memory issues we cannot anticipate. Students don't come to us with brains free from thought when they enter our classrooms, ready for our content to be the only thing in their minds. Students' lives are filled with all kinds of input that may be occupying their working memory without the teacher's knowledge. A student in your first-period class may have had an argument with their parent in the car. A student you teach after lunch may have eaten alone and wish they had more friends. Your last-period class may have several student-athletes who are already thinking about this afternoon's game. Several middle and high school teachers that I spoke to referenced having to overcome the material from the previous class that might still be sitting in a student's working memory. The debate that took place in their history class or the particularly challenging proof they just struggled through in geometry may still linger in their minds. Zane and Alyssa both said they engage in a "working memory purge." They might have students get out their mini-whiteboards and write silly things or draw a picture. They might ask them to rate how their day is going on a scale of one to ten. Neither spends a lot of time on this activity, but they feel it helps their students have a mental boundary between classes and clear their working memory of the previous lesson.

There's nothing you can do about the fact that other things will be competing with your content for student attention. What you can do is recognize when the student in front of you has reached the full line. Sometimes, the clues are subtle, like a student flipping through their book or notes with no evident destination. Other times, they are incredibly obvious, putting their head on their desk or explicitly saying, "I can't take anymore. My brain is full." An experienced teacher can sometimes feel a sense of mental overload being reached in the room by interpreting the behaviors associated with overload—fidgeting and squirming, staring into the middle distance, getting far too quiet, and giving answers that are seemingly unrelated to questions can all be signs that a student's brain needs a break. Hannah Eichhorst told me, "My students are usually game to try and not worry if they get something wrong, so if they aren't even willing to try, I know they are overloaded."

Experienced teachers have a plan for this moment. Perhaps, it is time for a couple of retrieval questions. Maybe, it is a good moment to throw in a little story or joke. Hannah sends them to get water. It could be time to stand up and summarize with their table mates. Notice that it doesn't have to be a full break that completely derails your class. It can just be a lighter moment to give time for their brains to leave focused mode for a short time. Zane has them take out their whiteboards and asks a question that is not related to his content, like "What's your favorite book?" He then asks a few easy academic questions. The final question gets them back to the content they were learning when the break began. Alyssa Powell told me, "When I see in their eyes that they are overloaded, I don't teach anything new for a bit. I take a 'review break,' asking them questions I know they'll get right." When they return to the day's content, that little bit of recovery allows them to refocus in a stronger way.

If the overload occurs because of the difficulty and complexity of the material, you may need to back up a little and take things step-by-step, practicing each before putting those parts together. Or it might be helpful to have a completely worked example somewhere students can reference. When I first started looking into worked examples, I was skeptical, wondering if those might increase the working memory demands because it shows steps the students are not yet on, but seeing the whole before tackling individual steps seems to help. Then, I thought about the time when people used maps rather than GPS devices. It was helpful to know the lay of the land while figuring out whether to turn right or left at a particular intersection, and this seems to be true with worked examples as well.

Of course, if a student finds that the worked example is causing him anxiety, he can always cover everything after the current step. Come to think of it, I sometimes did that with maps as well. I'd look at the whole route and then fold it into a smaller area. Steve Waltien, the actor I mentioned earlier, said he does the same thing when beginning to memorize a script. First, he reads the whole thing to see how all of the parts fit together. Then, he takes a sheet of paper and covers everything but the line he is working on to focus on it alone, already knowing how it fits into the whole story.

In the opening story of this chapter, I put Julia in the worst possible place a student can reach—catastrophic overload, the point at which a student has just frozen and won't be able to give an answer, no matter how much support is provided. I mentioned earlier that, because of a podcast, I now had techniques I could use to prevent what happened with Julia from happening again. I just heard the episode about six weeks too late. In Craig Barton's interview with Dylan William on the *Tips for Teachers* podcast, several suggestions are given to address situations like this one. Now, I might say, "Okay, I'll come back to you" and ask other students for an answer and then come back to the student to say "Do you agree." Dylan William suggests giving a "phone a friend" option where they can ask someone else and then either agree with their answer or augment it. I could have done something as simple as showing her a list of the four field forces to choose from. He says what is important is to not let "I don't know" be the end of the conversation, but there are quite a few ways to work around it rather than push them to a place of cognitive overload.

Cut yourself some slack. You are never going to manage this perfectly. You are going to overplan as you attempt to create desirable difficulty, taking kids right to their maximum without going over. Experienced teachers are better at avoiding the pitfalls simply because we have fallen into them so many times, but we never become perfect at it. It's not about becoming perfect; it's about being responsive to the cues in front of you and adapting to the present moment. Just keep paying attention, and you will find the challenge of managing student working memory easier.

Speaking of your attention, let me mention that the teacher's working memory can be taxed too. When you consider that you are teaching content, scanning the room for behavior and safety issues, checking for student understanding, and making observations about learning, you are likely to reach cognitive load at some point during every class period. It becomes easier after a few years because the content and the pedagogy with which you teach it are set in your long-term memory, and you will notice the difference in the mental energy you use when presenting it. Having learned something is very different from becoming fluid at teaching it. After a year of taking indoor cycle classes, I recently started teaching them, and the first time I practiced, I found it difficult to keep up with the instructions I was giving about pace and form while also timing moves. I would say we were going to engage in a climb for thirty seconds and then look down and see that we had been doing it for forty-five seconds. Don't worry. As things become

Some Techniques for Handling "I Don't Know"

(Definitely NOT a complete list - add your own!)

Come back to them
Make the question multiple choice
Allow student to "phone a friend" - Then augment their answer
Offer a clue (Starts with the letter "g")
Off your own answer and ask "True or False?"

Figure 1.1 Techniques for handling "I don't know."

embedded in long-term memory and you develop a deeply ingrained sense of how to teach a particular skill, you will have things chunked enough to help your own long-term memory.

Also, teachers can help themselves out with writing as it is a form of externalizing thoughts so they don't have to be held in working memory. It is the reason we make to-do lists, organize writing into outlines, and make concept maps. When Dmitiri Mendeleev was trying to find trends among the known elements, he wrote what was known about each one on a card and physically moved them around on the table to look for trends in an activity he called "chemical solitaire." You can take advantage of externalizing for yourself and your students as well. Writing the agenda on the board helps students with clarity, as I will discuss in Chapter 2, but it also helps the teacher to keep track of things without having to hold them in active memory. During the pandemic lockdown, I couldn't rely on the habits I had used for over twenty years, so I wrote out an outline each morning on a legal pad and kept it next to my computer. With so many other things taking up space in my working memory, this was a vital resource, and I have found it helpful to keep doing it since then. Doug Lemov gave good advice for teachers using writing in the management of their own working memory. He tweeted,

> If you write down observations as you circulate, your working memory will be free to be more responsive to students. And you won't forget what you observed. And if you write out the ideal answer you hope to get to a key question and carry it with you, on a clipboard, say, you can constantly refresh your own working memory about what you are hoping to see students write or talk about. And you can check it quickly. And this too will free your own working memory to observe better and to be more present with students.

Being present with students is vital to teaching, so do what you can to protect your working memory as well as theirs.

2 Clarity for Learning

I already mentioned that I take indoor cycling classes at my local YMCA. Every instructor approaches instruction differently. Some care about speed; others focus on tension level. Liz likes challenge blocks. She begins each class with an introduction in which she tells us exactly what we will be doing. "Today we have three challenges. One will be a set of rolling hills. Next is an endurance challenge. Then we'll end with sprints." As we get to each of those challenges, she gives us specific instructions, and she explains the benefits we will experience. At the end of an endurance challenge, she asks "Did you meet your goal? If not, did you stay motivated the whole time? That's what the goal is for." For the first few months of taking her class, I tried to figure out what her day job was. I was convinced that she was a fifth-grade teacher because she was so specific and so clear. It turned out that she raises money for nonprofit organizations, but at 6:00 p.m. on Mondays and Wednesdays, she is an educator. Her clarity taught me so much that I decided to become a cycling instructor myself, and while I combine elements from all of my instructors into my plans, I model the start of each class after Liz and her clarity speeches.

According to John Hattie's meta-analysis work, teacher clarity has a potential effect size of 0.75 if well implemented. Since the hinge point for highly effective techniques is 0.4, that's a huge impact; so it is worth exploring what clarity is and how we can take advantage of it in our classes. The nice thing about that is that, once you understand what it is, it may only require small tweaks to what you already do, not an overhaul of your whole pedagogy.

In their book *Clarity for Learning*, John Almarode and Kara Vandas outline three questions that both teachers and students should be able to answer at the outset of any learning experience.

1 What am I doing?
2 Why am I doing it?
3 How will I know when I have succeeded?

Starting a lesson with the answer to the first two questions is useful for students because they understand that there is purpose to what they are doing. One of my physics students, Max, told me that he finds it helpful to know how information will be used later. He said that he appreciates that his chemistry teacher didn't just tell him twenty ions to memorize by a certain date but instead explained that they would be using the ions to solve certain kinds of problems, and that they would need to know them by the quiz date so they could be used for that purpose from there on out. He said, "It's very beneficial to be shown how the facts and memorization aspects of the lesson will be applied ahead of time."

You might wonder why this is helpful. As long as a student can follow my instructions on a current task, why do they need to know the end result from the beginning? The answer is that it is difficult to arrive at a destination if you don't know what it is. If we were on a road trip, and someone asked "What are you doing?" I would be likely to answer with the destination. The answer might be, "I'm on my way to Yellowstone." It's unlikely that I would answer, "I'm driving a car."

If we got into a car, and you said to me, "You drive," I would immediately ask for the destination. It would be strangely aggressive if you said, "Don't worry about it. Just turn when I tell you to." Even if I agreed to a scenario like that, I would spend the entire trip feeling anxious because it is human nature to be interested in more than just the step we are currently taking. We instinctively know that the destination is what matters, not the means of reaching the destination, yet it can be easy to forget that as a teacher and ask students to start a task without knowing the purpose or what the evidence of their success will be.

If someone visits my classroom and asks my students what they are learning, will they answer with the destination or the process? Do they understand the part that matters? If not, it is likely that I have not properly communicated it to them and just hope they will trust me to give them instructions along the way. Will that leave them feeling anxious in my class in a way that could easily be prevented if I were more like my cycling instructor, Liz?

Perhaps what is needed is a shift in our thinking while we plan lessons. As a college student, I was required to make extremely detailed plans that explicitly laid out, not just the activities, but the logic about how my plan would meet the standards. The plan for one lesson was sometimes three pages long. I have never made a lesson plan with that level of specificity in my career, but being trained in that way of thinking was certainly helpful in my earliest years. As we become more comfortable and familiar with our content and our pedagogy, we often stop thinking this way and focus on what our students will do during our class. That's natural, but I wonder if lack of clarity for our students often comes from the fact that we have shifted our focus from the why to the how. I am certainly not suggesting that we go back to making multipage plans, but I am suggesting that we pause for a beat to reflect on why students are doing an activity and then communicate that to them.

In his book *Tips for Teachers*, math teacher and podcaster Craig Barton cautions against giving students the perception that your content is a series of disconnected topics. He rightly says, "Everything builds on something they (students) have encountered in the past, and everything is relevant to something they will encounter in the future." He uses a flow chart to show the connections, but that would certainly not be the only way to show connection. My head of school, Eric Bradley, was a history teacher before going into administration. He chose a broad theme to connect lessons to. It could have been the economy, art, religion, or the daily lives of citizens, but he spent the entire year circling back to that theme with each event or movement they studied. In science, that could be a difficult approach as the deeper threads require a massive amount of knowledge to be acquired before they can be seen. A science teacher could, however, keep pointing to the progress made by scientists. We could continually ask, "How did this build on what came before?" and "How do you think this impacted future discoveries?" When I taught the periodic table, I often made an analogy to learning to read, saying, "First, we learned the letters (the elements), and then we made words (compounds). Now, we are going to put them into sentences (chemical reaction equations)." The method is less important than the idea that clarity can be achieved when students see how the individual pieces of what they are learning fits into the bigger picture.

Clarity, when implemented well, has a direct link to motivation. It is difficult for a student to maintain hard work in learning if they only understand what they are supposed to do without any understanding of why. As John Almarode and Kara Vandas put it, "If we don't provide clarity about what learners are expected to learn from a specific task, activity, or strategy, learners will most likely view these events as exercises that simply require compliance." They will get the activity done and check it off of their to-do list, but they will be unlikely to make the learning connections for themselves. If the activity is difficult, they will lose motivation quickly without "the why," just as we would. High school junior Kate told me, "Science is like a bunch of facts swimming around until it is anchored to the bigger picture." She has determined that a good science teacher frequently connects the specific thing they are teaching in the moment with the way it fits in conjunction with the previous lecture or upcoming unit. In her book on the spiritual practice of Sabbath, author J. Dana Trent said, "It's the why of a thing that keeps it relevant." She's right about that for spiritual disciplines, and it is just as important for academic work. Without "the why," a task is just a task. With it, the task becomes a mission.

In a study of 120 undergraduate students, Canadian researchers Susan Rodger, Harry Murray, and Anne Cummings found a correlation between classes with high levels of teacher clarity and higher levels of motivation and self-efficacy, resulting in improved achievement on subsequent tests. While they drew no conclusions about why this is true, the answer may be as obvious as the idea that knowing where you are going and how to get there is more motivating than hoping you will arrive at an unknown destination. Is the reduction of stress, and thus working memory load, the reason why teacher clarity matters so much? Maybe, it is the sense of independence we get from clarity that helps us learn. Perhaps it is because it is difficult to be motivated by seemingly unrelated steps if we don't see how they fit into the whole scheme. I'm willing to bet it is an interaction of all of these possibilities.

In their article for *Higher Education*, Josipa Roksa and her colleagues found a causal relationship between clarity and motivation—teacher credibility. Their article concludes, "When students experience greater exposure to clear and organized instruction, they perceive their faculty as being more invested in their learning and development, and they report being more academically motivated and engaged in their studies." Clarity, it seems, communicates to students that teachers take their job seriously and instills more confidence in the minds of their students.

Effective feedback during an activity is a form of clarity as it helps students on the path of that third question, "How will I know when I have succeeded?" In their book *Uncommon Sense Teaching*, Barbara Oakley, Beth Rogowsky, and Terrence Sejnowski discuss the role of formative assessment in teacher and student clarity. They say, "Teachers and students alike know their final destination, but what proof do they have that they've reached it? Enter formative and summative assessments. Formative assessments are markers along the path that indicate a student's progress." We'll discuss more about formative assessment in the final chapter, but it is at its most powerful when used as a form of feedback for both students and teachers.

Of course, if feedback is going to be useful, it must be given while there is still time to act on it. Telling students at the end of the activity that they have done something wrong has some value and is what we would do in a summative assessment. If, however, we want students to succeed while practicing a skill, they need some form of feedback at each step, and they need time to adjust their course when they have gone astray. Providing high quality feedback and the time to apply it will produce better learning. In his book *The New Science of Learning*, Todd Zakrajsek calls feedback "a game plan for getting better," but students can only follow that plan if the activity isn't over. They must have time to implement the feedback that can ultimately lead to clarity or they will just hear that they are wrong and not that they can improve.

Interestingly, in their article "The Power of Feedback," in the *Review of Educational Research*, John Hattie and Helen Timperley identify three questions that feedback needs to answer in order to be effective, and they sound a lot like the three clarity questions. They are

1. Where am I going?
2. How am I going?
3. What do I do next?

Andy Tharby calls this "identifying your throughline," and I really like that as a way of thinking about the lesson, the chapter, the unit, and the semester. There is some thread that is connecting all of it, and knowing that makes a difference to how you communicate it to your students. I would never teach the chapter on bonding before teaching the chapter on the periodic table because I know they will need to use the periodic table frequently to determine bond type and to look up charges when writing ionic formulas. I know the reason for the chapter order, but do my students know? It may not be necessary for them to know the rationale for everything, but they might be more motivated to understand the details of the periodic table if I have told them just how much they will use it later.

Since clarity influences both motivation and achievement, let's look at practical ways we can help our students know what they are doing, why they are doing it, and how they will know where they are on the path to success.

If you spend any amount of time in online teacher forums, you will find a lot of mockery of the idea that the learning objective should be written on the board. I know that many administrators have gone too far with this expectation, requiring that "I can" statements be posted around the room for every activity. Like most requirements, however, it begins with a good intention. As we have seen, making the learning outcome clear for both the teacher and the student is important. Writing the objective on the board, however, is not the only way to make it clear. In fact, if you don't simplify the objective into student-friendly language, posting the objective on the board may actually make your lesson less clear.

Regardless of the delivery method, it is vital that students know the objective of their learning. In their *Framework for Intentional and Targeted Teaching*, Douglas Fisher, Nancy Frey, and Stefani Hite describe why it is important for the purpose to be clarified for students at the outset of instruction. Not only does it help teachers to know how to check for understanding, but knowing the relevance of the content helps motivate students to be responsible for their learning. Children don't respond to their parents well when they ask why they need to do something and the parent answers, "Because I said so." Without clarity, students may feel that is the implicit answer the teacher is giving them to the question they are always asking, even if it is not always asked aloud, "Why do I need to learn this?" However you choose to communicate it, communicate it clearly.

So, how can we make clarity happen? We can start by answering the question most students ask as they enter class. What are we doing today? My high school physics teacher, Jim Barbara, had a little section of the board that simply said, "Today we will ..." and listed the activities we would be doing. I loved that, at any point in the lesson, I could look up and see where we were and what remained. Since students walk through the door asking what they are doing today, my board has a beefed-up version of Mr. Barbara's. It includes the bellwork, the objective, the day's agenda, and announcements. I write the objective as a question because I believe it unconsciously stimulates curiosity. While I do it to communicate with students, it benefits me too because it acts as an aid to my working memory since I can check to see what comes next without having to remember.

I think most teachers answer the first question fairly well on a daily basis. Fewer teachers regularly answer the second question—why are we doing what we are doing?—very well. Perhaps this is due to the curse of expertise—because we think the reason is evident. We forget that we know the curriculum goals, and the students do not. We don't consider the fact that they weren't involved in the planning of the lesson. Yet, for all of us, understanding why we are doing what we are asked to do is critical to our willingness to sustain the work involved.

There are many ways to communicate purpose. With elementary students, we usually take the explicit approach, explaining the purpose of the activity and what we want them to learn from it. With high school and college students, we might put it in the syllabus. We can also take the approach taken by the middle school teacher you met in the previous chapter, Hannah Eichhorst. She says, "Students don't listen when I tell them, so I have them tell me." After she tells students what they will be doing, she asks, "What do you think is the purpose? Why are we doing this?" After a few responses, there will be a student whose answer matches hers, and she can build on their response to make sure they understand why they are learning the skill they are learning that day. What I love about that practice is that she communicates every day that there is a purpose and asks them to think about what it might be prior to doing it. Alyssa Powell told me that her communication is ongoing. She continually returns to the reason for the objective throughout the lesson. As they change activity, she reminds them of that day's purpose. "Remember, we are learning how to predict cold fronts today" helps them make connections between multiple activities that they may otherwise view as unrelated.

What I think most of us have not done well on a regular basis is provide students with the way they can know if they have succeeded with a task. As I conducted interviews with science teachers for this book, this is the question that elicited more blank stares than any other. Outside of a few key lessons, I struggle with it myself. It is important, though, so let's address it in more detail.

First, you have to envision how *you* will know if a student has been successful. That's probably not hard if you plan to grade the task because you know what you will be looking for. If it is an in-class activity that you don't plan to grade, it may require more thought. As you design the task, ask yourself what you hope students will be able to do (skill) or explain (content) at the end of the experience. After that, it's just a matter of being explicit about what the end result looks like and any milestones in reaching that end. Putting those milestones in writing will allow them to check their own progress rather than having you repeat it frequently. Andy Tharby sums it up well when he says, "Success criteria should, where possible be written in the imperative and couched in measurable, everyday language." Students don't need the educational jargon we find in state standards. They need to know what they are expected to do and to learn. For example, when solving a circuit problem in my physics class, I do not use the standard outlined by my state, which says they should, "analyze systems with multiple potential differences and resistors connected in series and parallel circuits, both conceptually and mathematically, in terms of voltage, current and resistance." If I do, they will be more confused than they were when we started. Instead, I tell them what I want them to be able to do. I say, "Today, you will calculate the voltage and current for each of the six resistors in this combination circuit." Because they know the goal, I can teach them the process without bogging them down in words like "systems" and "both conceptually and mathematically."

When teaching the writing of chemical formulas for ionic bonds, chemistry teacher Melanie Dunning provides the details of what is happening with the electrons first, using dot diagrams and arrows to physically move the electrons from the cation to the anion. Not only does that help the method of formula writing make more sense and provide them with a secondary method, it also gives them a criterion for success because she can say, "You aren't done until you run out of dots and spaces." About halfway through their practice activity, she puts the key under the visualizer. That way students can check themselves. If they have gotten it wrong, they may be able to recognize what they did wrong themselves or check in with a classmate about why their answer is different from the key as she circulates the room doing some individual reteaching. In Alyssa Powell's meteorology unit on global winds, she does some direct instruction first. Then, at the start of a mapping activity, she gives them a way to check maps online. As she circulates, she is able to tell who has the concept figured out and who still needs support. She points to the spot in their notes or book that will be helpful in completing the task. In a lab with a complicated setup, my students find the diagram hard to follow, so I set up a model and place it at the back of the lab to help them reproduce it.

Imagine you are doing an activity about lab tools. You should introduce the activity with a statement like,

> At the end of the period, I want you to be able to identify the specific purpose of ten pieces of lab equipment, so you will know how to use

the right tool for the purpose in experiments. Scientists made these with their purpose in mind and know when to use different types of tools to accomplish those purposes. Remember, I don't just want you to know the name of it; I also want you to be able to explain its purpose.

As you circulate the room, pick up a graduated cylinder and ask, "What is this used for?" If they just name the piece of equipment, remind them that, while it is good to know the names of things, the purpose of today's activity is to know the purpose. Then ask them when they would use it in an experiment. They need to be reminded frequently of both the purpose and the success criteria.

One mistake I often make is to affirm them too quickly when they are only partially correct. For example, if they respond that the purpose of a graduated cylinder is to measure the volume of liquids, I might be quick to say yes. But there are several pieces of equipment that do that, and each exists for a different reason, so I really want a more specific answer. Grab a beaker and an Erlenmeyer flask and say, "All three of these measure liquid volume. How are they different?" If you want them to be specific, require that in their answers. It feels pedantic, but if you want a specific result, you must require it. There is nothing wrong with telling a student they are almost right or partially correct. Science is extremely detailed, and it is good for them to understand that tiny differences, like whether a number is a subscript or a superscript, often matter a great deal.

You, as the teacher, probably have to be more specific than you think you do, to the point where it feels like you are going overboard. When students balance chemical equations, they wander into a lot of wrong ways to meet the big goal of making reactants match products. Novices don't understand enough about compounds to realize that H_2O (water) is very different from H_2O_2 (hydrogen peroxide) and that changing the formula makes a different compound. So, to provide clarity about the goal, you have to be extra specific and frequently remind them of the conditions for success. Instead of only saying, "The number of atoms on the right side must match the number on the left side," you may want to head the paper with, "The number of atoms on the right side must match the number on the left side by changing ONLY the coefficients."

Zane Smitley teaches ninth-grade biology, so his class is the first experience they have with formal lab reports. While they have learned graphing in math classes, it is different when representing scientific data, so he spends a lot of time preparing them for proper graph construction. He provides model graphs and a checklist both on paper and in the school's learning management system. They should know when they hand in their lab report if their graph is properly constructed because he has given them all the criteria required for success. I love watching him interact with students when they ask him to check something before they turn it in. He never just says, "This is wrong. Do this instead." He draws the mistake out of them saying, "Why did you do it this way? What do you think is missing? Does that answer the question that was asked?" It takes more time, but getting them to a point of realization on their own helps them identify their own success in future assignments.

To us, this feels awkward. It seems like we will come off as condescending if we are that specific, especially if we do it multiple times. We would be bothered if an administrator did this in faculty meetings, but that's because they are usually talking to us about things we already know or things we have done before. We just need a quick reminder or notice of change. In the reality of teaching a classroom filled with novice learners, it does not feel condescending. It helps students become more independent because they can check for themselves whether they have been successful. I repeat instructions very frequently. To me, it feels like a lot, but I've never had a student tell me that I repeat things too much. Zane's students don't ever come to me and say, "I wish he had given me fewer examples of graphs." But many students complain about teachers who don't clearly model. Certainty is motivating; uncertainty is demotivating.

Providing clarity in print form will prevent you from having to repeat yourself so much. They don't have all of this in their long-term memories yet, and the working memory is slippery. If you are relying on verbal instructions, they will ask you to repeat yourself frequently. If you put it on paper or project it on the wall or write it on the board, they can check for themselves at any point in the process. When you circulate and see a student is balancing equations incorrectly by crossing out and writing new subscripts, you can simply point at the word coefficients at the top of the page.

One of the goals of clarity is to give students the ability to judge their progress for themselves. If the teacher has to stand by and give a constant stream of feedback, the student will not develop independence in their learning. The teacher needs to provide enough information about success criteria that a student can judge their own progress as they move toward their learning goal. We don't want students floundering without our help.

If they are, it is probably a sign that we have not provided them with clear ways to identify their issues or the tools to solve them. But we also shouldn't hover. Too much feedback can lead a student to believe they know how to do something when the teacher was really doing it for them.

It may be useful to share an example from outside the academic world, so let's head back to the YMCA. A few months after I started taking cycle classes, I began setting goals about distance, tension level, and power on the bike. At first, I only knew how to check these statistics at the end of the class. I was often surprised to get to the end of a workout and find that I hadn't achieved as much distance as I thought. Because I wasn't tracking that information during the class, I didn't have the ability to make adjustments that would help me reach my goals. I could do better on a different day, but I didn't know how to do better at the moment. Then, an instructor showed me how to use the bike's computer to see real-time information during class. It was tempting to stay on that screen. We like having constant access to information, but I quickly learned that was unwise. It made me so focused on the numbers that I couldn't pay attention to instructions. Worse, I was so focused on the numbers that I couldn't enjoy doing the things that would improve the numbers, and I was in a state of panic if the average didn't move as quickly as I thought it should. Worst of all, I wasn't building any internal sense of how to improve because I was relying too much on the bike itself rather than how my legs felt or how hard I was working. Eventually, I disciplined myself to only visit that screen once every four minutes. That gave me enough information to figure out what I need to do to make progress for the next check, but it didn't do my thinking for me.

I also found this to be true when I was the yearbook advisor. I didn't check progress on a page in the first three weeks unless a student asked me to because the creative process isn't linear. Page design often involved putting things in, hating them, deleting them, starting over, and adjusting colors or fonts. Judging it too early in that process led to vanilla pages. Judging it too late often meant a complete redesign, which no one wanted. I did my first review of their first deadline pages after a month. One year, I had a student who wanted to plant herself right next to me and ask about every line and image she inserted. It was driving me crazy, and I knew it was coming from her insecurity, so I finally said, "I'm not looking at one thing at a time. Go do five things. You can only show it to me after you have five things in place."

As you try to find the sweet spot for your students, ask yourself questions about their age and the complexity of your content. We need to check in with them frequently enough to notice if they need some adjustment, but we shouldn't judge each number they write as they write it. Come back to the clarity questions. Do they know what they are doing and why they are doing it? Are they able to gauge their own progress? It's a moving target, but aiming for clarity will serve you and your students well.

3 Prior Knowledge and Schema

At the start of any new chapter, I start with some introduction questions. What do you already know about waves? What is an atom? Can any of you explain how to throw a curveball? What do you think holds a plane in the air? Here's one that has played out the same way for all twenty-five years of my physical science teaching.

Me: "What's the first thing you think of when I say the word 'acid'?"
Students: "Dangerous. Burns skin. Eats through anything. Green. Melting flesh."
Me: "Okay, some of that is true of very strong acids—except green. I don't know of any acids that are green; I think that just comes from cartoons. Would it surprise you to know that you eat acids almost every day?"
Students: "What?"
Me: "Ketchup is an acid. Orange juice—pretty much all fruits. Next question, what do you think of when I say the word 'base?'"
Students: "Foundation of something. Baseball. Softball. The bottom. Something essential."
Me: "Do you know there are chemical bases? Or maybe you've heard the word 'alkali.'"
Them: "... Huh?"

While their understanding of acids is distorted by pop culture, they do have some concept of what an acid is and what it does. Bases aren't used in cartoons, books, or movies, except for the silent movie version of *The Phantom of the Opera* and one rather disturbing scene in *Fight Club*, so they don't have any prior connection to them. When I start giving examples of bases in their everyday lives, they struggle to understand how they fit into the same category.

Until I started learning about cognitive science, I didn't know what a powerful tool these start-of-chapter questions were. I had been using them to spark curiosity and to find out what they already knew about the topic I was preparing to teach. It helped me know where to start and identify prior misconceptions. It wasn't until recently that I recognized I was activating their prior relevant knowledge to help build their schema. Their acid schema needs work, but until I start drawing out some of their knowledge about household cleaners and medications, they don't even know they have a schema for bases.

In *Why Don't Students Like School*, Daniel Willingham explains how background knowledge helps us comprehend passages we read. He says, "We don't take in new information in a vacuum. We interpret new things we read in light of other information we already have on the topic." This makes perfect sense. We will understand a passage about knitting much more if we already understand that purl is a verb that someone who is encountering that word for the first time.

In my university methods courses, I was taught to activate prior knowledge, but I was not taught how it aided learning. Activating prior knowledge is important because newly learned information will be tied to already known information, like a sort of neurological velcro. This tie is powerful, so you don't want to activate just any knowledge they have; you want to activate knowledge that is relevant to the lesson you are about to teach. In their article "Increasing Comprehension by Activating Prior Knowledge," William Christen and Thomas Murphy explain the importance of having and activating prior knowledge. They say it is the only way to get past memorization of bits and pieces, stating, "Prior knowledge is an essential element in the quest for making meaning." Since making meaning is our ultimate goal as educators, this is obviously a critical practice that we want to do well.

Activating prior knowledge starts with bringing it to the forefront of their minds, but the process does not end there. As Kevin Washburn says in *The Architecture of Learning*, "Connecting new sensory data and prior knowledge requires more than putting the two within cognitive reach of each other." It takes work to explicitly make connections between what is known and what is being learned, but it is valuable to build a student's schema for a given topic.

Think about your lesson. Where might their experience be related? Make a list and write questions about those things. If you are going to teach physics students about the distance traveled by projectiles fired at various angles, you can ask them about golf, volleyball, and basketball, but it is also valuable to have them remember how the sine and cosine of angles affect the horizontal and vertical components of a vector and discuss that at the beginning of the lesson. Both are part of their past learning, but they may not yet be connected into a schema.

So, what is schema? The short answer is that it is everything you know that is related to any given topic, but it is a bit more layered than that. If we look at a few descriptions from different scholars, we can see how complex it is. George Mason University researcher Sharon Alayne Widmayer describes it as "categorical rules or scripts that we use to interpret the world" and says that "new information is processed according to how it fits into these rules, called schema." In their book *Uncommon Sense Teaching*, Barbara Oakley, Beth Rogowsky and Terry Sejnowski describe schema as "a set of neural shelves that holds together the different sets of links that a student is learning about a subject." In *The New Science of Learning*, UNC professor Todd Zakrajsek says, "As you interact with the world around you, your brain puts similar information together." Looking at all of these descriptions together, we can conclude that, while schema is everything you know about a topic, it is also the unconscious rules and relationships your brain has assigned to what you know and how those facts relate to each other.

When it comes to understanding schema, I find a metaphor helpful. Imagine a photograph you might find at your grandparents' house—a real, physical one that you can hold in your hands. When you turn it over, someone has written on the back. She may have written the date, the event, and the names of the people in the photo. That represents a limited schema about that picture. If you asked her to tell you the story of the event, you might be able to grow that schema by writing more detail on the back side of the photo or including a scrap of paper inside the frame. A good scrapbooker might be able to add context to that photo by grouping a few together on a nicely themed page. That photograph, however, only exists in one place, so the schema is difficult to use when searching for it. If I wanted to reference it elsewhere, I would have limited results because I would need to go to my grandmother's house and turn the photo over. In the same way, while learning, a limited schema will produce limited results.

Now, imagine a photo you have stored in the cloud. When you uploaded the photo, the metadata about time and location were automatically recorded. Facial recognition likely tagged the photo, which you could then augment. If you were really on top of things, you added tags like "birthday party, Papa, and Bob's house." If you do this with lots of photos, you have created an overlapping, interconnected network of photographs. And it is searchable within any category you choose. You may have hundreds of photos from multiple events at Bob's house. If you have properly tagged each photo, you can bring them all up at once to make a scrapbook of Bob's hospitality. If you are looking for all the pictures you have of your Papa, you can bring all of them up from many dates, occasions, and locations by searching for his tag. This is more representative of a real schema, overlapping and interconnected "tags" of our knowledge.

The value of connecting new content to existing schema cannot be overestimated. Widmayer states, "Information that does not fit into these schema may not be comprehended, or may not be comprehended correctly. This is the reason why readers have a difficult time comprehending a text on a subject they are not familiar with even if the person comprehends the meaning of the individual words in the passage." The frustration caused by not having schema to connect to might even cause us to give up on learning as we are unlikely to continue reading a passage we don't understand because we no longer have the mental shortcut that aids our thinking.

How about a nonacademic example? When I shop at the grocery store, I know where to find the peanut butter because in most grocery stores, it is on the same aisle as bread. There is one store I don't visit often where it is kept in the produce department, and I find it unsettling. Because it doesn't fit into my grocery store schema, it takes extra mental effort to find it in that store. In early 2020, I was irritated that my local Walmart changed its layout. Because it takes time to learn, I had not yet developed a new schema for this previously familiar place when we entered lockdown. When the time came to reenter the store a few months later, I didn't want to. I have shopped there very little since then because I don't have the motivation to rebuild that schema.

Zakrajsek goes on to say that, as your schemas grow and become more complex, it is easier to incorporate more information into them because you are connecting into an already existing neural structure without having to build the knowledge from scratch. In her 2023 keynote address at the Learning and the Brain conference, Oakley suggested that "a good schema can serve as the equivalent of a bigger working memory capacity" because it allows you to draw from a variety of interrelated information, which then has the ability to activate other information, like falling dominoes. If I had never been in any grocery store, I wouldn't have a clue where to begin looking for the peanut butter, but as I go to a few with slightly different layouts, I can better predict where to find it in unfamiliar stores, as long as they aren't drastically different from those I know.

I can hear you saying, "Okay, I'm on board with this idea. We have to build schema. But how?" Let's look at a number of practical ways that this can be applied in your classroom tomorrow.

Because no concept is only one thing, the schema keeps growing every time a student learns something new. As you teach Newton's laws of motion, a student may activate their knowledge of basketball, race car driving, or their cat running madly around their house. Some students may connect with all three. This is why students who have many rich and varied activities learn more than those with limited experiences. They simply have more in their schema to connect with. Students who read widely, visit museums, and listen to a wide variety of music have more to connect with than those who obsess over only one activity. If you are in a school where it is appropriate, encourage parents to expose their students to as many rich experiences as possible. But recognize that you will teach students who have not had those opportunities, so you may need to provide more for them. Otherwise, you are trying to build on top of a foundation that is either weak or doesn't exist at all. While it would be impractical to think you can take a lot of field trips, there are many options for virtual museum tours and trips that they can do during class or for homework.

The second thing that is valuable has become controversial—have students memorize knowledge. To be valuable for schema building, knowledge must be firmly in the long-term memory and then brought into conscious thought at the right time. That means students must memorize enough things to have prior knowledge. I'm not saying they have to memorize everything, but they must have a knowledge base within themselves from which to draw. There will be more on how to decide what should be memorized in Chapter 8, but having knowledge in long-term memory is the only way to build schema. Daniel Willingham said it well in his article "How Knowledge Helps." He said, "Knowledge is not only cumulative, it grows exponentially. Those with a rich base of factual knowledge find it easier to learn more—the rich get richer. In addition, factual knowledge enhances cognitive processes like problem solving and reasoning. The richer the knowledge base, the more smoothly and effectively these cognitive processes—the very ones that teachers target—operate."

If you want students to think about the right things during your lesson, you must help them bring their knowledge from long-term memory into their conscious thought. That happens mostly through questioning and prompts. Douglas Fisher and Nancy Frey recommend a variety of methods for schema building using prompts. They identify four types of prompts in *Checking for Understanding*—background knowledge, process and procedure, reflection, and heuristic.

Background knowledge is asking students to use what they already know to help them with current knowledge acquisition. You activate this by asking questions related to things they have learned before that are germane to the current task. For example, as you teach earth science students how to predict weather after having learned to read a weather map, you can ask "What is the symbol for a cold front?" and "What does it mean when we see both triangles and circles?" Because they have learned it before, bringing it back to their consciousness just before they need to use it is essential for engaging in the higher-level thinking needed for prediction.

Process and procedure prompts involve reminding students of the steps or guidelines for a problem being solved or prediction being made. When physics students learn force analysis, it goes more smoothly if they follow a specific order, first addressing weight and then applied force before calculating normal force and then friction. It isn't because a rule says they must be solved that way; it just leads to less confusion because applied force and weight influence normal force, and friction is proportional to normal force. Doing it in a different order will simply lead to more bewilderment about how to proceed. I write the order of the steps on my board and refer often to why the order helps, hoping it will build their schema for the relationships among physical forces.

Reflective prompts are asking students to reflect on their own thinking. At the end of calorimetry problems in which we solve for equilibrium temperature, I usually ask "Does this answer make sense?" Students jump to say yes before I have even finished asking the question because they know that should be the right answer. I pause and ask, "What did you look at to see if it made sense?" After a few blank stares, I walk them through how they might recognize if the answer didn't make sense—The equilibrium temperature must be between the two original temperatures, and it will likely be closer to the one that had more mass or a higher specific heat capacity. They don't like investing time in doing it, but those who do are more likely to catch errors earlier in the process during the next problem. And I know when they have because they will approach me with a problem and say, "I know something is off because this answer is higher than it should be, but I'm not sure what I did wrong."

Heuristic prompts can help students with their schema because it allows them to create informal processes of their own. The teacher can guide their thinking with questions like "How might you go about ...?" and confirming whether their idea is likely to work. In biology, Zane Smitley has a project in which students hypothesize about the yield of plants. They are then required to grow plants using their hypothesis, but first they must design their experiment, accounting for how they will implement their variable, how they will measure progress, and how they will display their results. Doing this requires them to draw on a lot of their previously learned knowledge and to extend it into this new context. This is big-time schema building.

In a 2021 report, the Education Endowment Foundation recommended an additional strategy for schema building—concept mapping. "It is thought this approach may help pupils receive, organize, and extend schematic knowledge of a topic in a more efficient way, encouraging connections between related items of learning." In a way, the creation of a concept map is bringing a student's schema from inside their head to a sheet of paper, helping them to see the connections in a new way and strengthening the schema in their minds. Consider using any or all of these prompts to aid students in schema construction.

Activating prior knowledge usually involves using a lot of examples that fit into the new concept being learned, particularly simple ones with which most students will already be familiar. This means the teacher needs to have varied interests in order to pull from a variety of sources in their own lives or the lives of those around them. The teacher who constantly pays attention during any experience can store away examples from home, church, vacations, concerts, television shows, and the conversations they overhear for use in the explanation of concepts. This isn't easy because it means constantly being aware, but the benefits to schema building are strong enough to make it worth the effort. Andy Tharby calls designing good examples "an art form in its own right" and acknowledges that it is not easy, taking years for an experienced teacher to hone and develop. I love the way he describes the benefits when he writes, "Effective examples not only bring insight and clarity, but ... they can inject a topic with emotion, humor, absurdity, poignancy, or a sense of the unexpected. They breathe new life into potentially stagnant ideas." My experience has also been that providing examples from my own experiences and allowing students to provide examples from theirs helps us to understand each other better as people, making learning in the classroom a warmer experience.

Because I teach middle and high school students, I know that they have some experience that is related to almost every topic I teach them. I start new chapters with the type of questions I described earlier, but I start all lessons with lead-in questions to intentionally bring up relevant prior knowledge and have them respond on their mini-whiteboards. These questions usually involve asking them to generate examples because they have to think deeply about what is related to the concept I've given them. It gives me a wide variety of access points for my teaching, and it allows me to identify whether they have brought up irrelevant prior knowledge.

The biology teacher Zane Smitley said that most of his freshman students have little academic experience with what he is about to teach, outside of a basic level sixth-grade life science class. Because of that lack of experience, he starts with questions that don't seem related to academic content, including things about the food they eat or exercises they do. This allows him to bring up prior knowledge they have about plants or oxygen consumption in a familiar context before connecting them to concepts like photosynthesis and respiration. In his anatomy classes, it's pretty easy to bring up relevant prior knowledge about their bodies because they are sitting there with them, and all he has to do is direct their awareness or ask questions about activities in which those bones and muscles have been used. One of his anatomy students, Kathryn, used to tell me about going home and petting her cat as she described all of the muscles she had learned about during dissection. Making those connections with her real, living pet intertwined academic content with her already existing schema.

One thing I have noticed since using mini-whiteboards for this practice in my own classes is that students activate each other's prior knowledge in ways I cannot because of generational differences. While answering those preliminary questions, they may reference a song or streaming show that I haven't even heard of (because I'm middle-aged, and they are not). I'll ask them to explain it to me, but other students benefit from their shared schema.

Hannah Eichhorst takes advantage of YouTube to activate prior knowledge with her middle schoolers. She shows them a video that is seemingly unrelated to that day's lesson and asks them to make observations and inferences, guiding them using their own answers.

Alyssa Powell uses KWL charts for schema building. Students fill in the "Know" part of the chart with what they already know about a topic. The "Want to Know" section is a great place for students to ask questions. The "Learned" section is often neglected for time. The best thing about the KWL chart is its flexibility; it can be done individually or in small groups or as an entire class, and I can change it up based on the needs of the group in front of me. I have one section that gets off task quickly, so I'm not going to divide them into groups and send them off to fill in charts. For that class, this is a quiet individual activity. I have another class that is a little too quiet, wanting to be told exactly what to do at each step. I want them to interact a bit more, so for them, this is a whole-class activity in which I write down what they are calling out. It's also a great bellwork activity. No matter how you do it, having them write what they know and what they would like to know is helpful in building schema.

If you are in a school where you can communicate with the teachers your students have had at prior levels, you should spend some time together. In my school, I teach physical science to all eighth-grade students. When Melanie Dunning gets them in chemistry, she knows what they should know from my class because we are right across the hall from each other and spend a great deal of nerd time talking about what we teach. She knows that I have spent significant time on electronegativity, which makes it easier for her to teach the difference between ionic and covalent bonding. When I get some of them back in physics, I know that they have been taught intermolecular forces and can reference that when we talk about the high specific heat capacity of water.

The scope and sequence of curricula, when executed well, should be an ongoing process of schema building. If you can make connections to the curricula of other disciplines, even better. The art teacher practices a lot of chemistry, so go to her, for examples, that might help build the schema of students she has had before you. When teaching vectors and projectiles in physics, it is going to be helpful to know what the math teachers have taught students about sine, cosine, and tangent or whether they have played badminton in PE (Physical Education). There are a lot of Latin roots in science, so have a chat with the ELA (English Language Arts) and foreign language teachers in your building. The more connections you can help students make to other disciplines, the more complex their schema will become, and science is often the place where they meet.

When it comes to teaching chemistry, physics, and physical science, do yourself a favor and identify your athletes and artists early. Swimmers are amazing at explaining how each stroke works, and you can connect them to Newton's laws and kinematics. Runners know that they don't stop immediately upon reaching the finish line, and gymnasts can explain why it is difficult to "stick the landing." You can take advantage of both of those examples when teaching about the relationship between impulse, force, and time. Artists have experience with pigment mixing and color on which you can build while discussing the frequency of light. Explaining oxidation is easier when at least one student has glazed pottery in one color in order to make it come out the way they want it after it has been fired in the kiln. This is all part of their schema as individuals, but you can help it become part of their collective schema as a class.

Be careful when activating prior knowledge to avoid activating nonrelevant knowledge. It may seem fun and engaging to connect the point you are making to a Taylor Swift song, but you will unwittingly take up space in the working memory of your students that your content will then have to compete with. I'm not saying to avoid pop culture references altogether because it is a good way of building relationships with your students if you are genuinely interested in some of the same things they are. I am saying that it would be better to save that analogy or example for the end of the lesson.

Another thing to be careful about when activating prior knowledge is to look out for prior misconceptions. When it comes to science, there are many. Students have only been partially taught some things as their teachers judiciously omitted some details to save working memory capacity. Some students have been influenced by politics and scientific skepticism or simply missed an important detail while learning a concept in the past. Some students blend some real science knowledge with inaccurate ideas presented in television and movies. If we don't find the misconceptions at the outset of our lesson, the new knowledge we are teaching might be connected to a wrong idea. Misconceptions tend to be stubborn, like words I learned to spell wrong and still have to rely on autocorrect to help me with. In their book *Checking for Understanding*, Fisher and Frey suggest pausing occasionally during a lesson to ask students to summarize what they have just heard, explain a concept, or predict an outcome. If we carefully word our questions, we can find out whether they have activated relevant and accurate prior knowledge and incorporated the new information accurately. After a few years of teaching a topic, you will have a good idea of what the common errors are and can construct your checks for understanding with the intent of finding those.

We need some techniques for correcting misconceptions because we don't want to embarrass students and reduce their desire to learn. The seventh-grade teacher Hannah Eichhorst told me that she often has two lists on the board for their answers. For example, she might be teaching about things that have cells. The question she asks is "What is an example of something that has cells?" When her students give answers like trees and dogs, she puts them in the category of things that have cells. When a student says, "a computer," she says, "Okay, that is something that does not have cells. Thanks for helping me build that list." All students' answers are on the board and all feel they have contributed to the discussion; no one was embarrassed even when they were wrong. That would be difficult to do with more nuanced information, but it works great for things with a definite boundary. I've done something similar with energy types. I have seven types of energy listed on the board. I hold a picture of a runner and ask which type that would fit under. The answer I am looking for is "kinetic," but often a student will say "elastic potential." Rather than saying no, I ask them to explain why they think so. Runners know how important the knees and ankles are to running and accurately think of that as part of the process. I then put the runner into both categories because that is not an error; it is an acknowledgement of complexity in science.

When I asked Alyssa Powell how she responds to students with misconceptions, she said that she often says, "I understand why you might think that. Let's circle back to it after we learn this." I love that because it values the thought process and the participation, but it sends the message that they are probably wrong and are about to learn differently. Since my students are a bit older, I do tell them they are wrong, but since I still want them to feel free to participate without fear, I say something like, "Umm, not really, but thank you for playing" while giving them a wink and a smile. After a few answers establish a pattern, I come back to that student to see if they have another thought, and they usually do.

How we frame the initial question might elicit better answers, so we want to carefully consider our approach. If it is too open-ended, we get unrelated answers. For example, I love teaching about how the characteristics of sound waves influence what we hear. For years, I started that class with a very open-ended prompt, "Tell me some words you might use to describe a sound." This was frustrating because I was looking for words like "deep, loud, raspy," but I was getting answers like "weird and creepy." Two years ago, I made one simple adjustment. I stated it almost the same way, "Tell me some words you might use to describe *how something sounds, for example high pitched*." That simple word change and example gave me much better initial responses that I could build off of, adding a question about whether that qualitative word (loud) could be made quantitative (90 db). My musicians then recognized that high-pitched could be specific "A sharp above middle C" or "356 Hz." Don't be afraid to ask leading questions. They are novice learners, and their brains need help pulling up the appropriate schema.

I hope I haven't strayed too far from the point about activating prior knowledge, but I do want to make sure we all understand that not all prior knowledge will be accurate or relevant. The learner's brain will activate some kind of prior knowledge whether you ask it to or not, so plan your prompts carefully to get relevant and accurate prior knowledge to connect with and build schema in a helpful way.

4 Focus and Diffuse Modes

When I was ten years old, I was in the car with my mom and brother. We were on a three-hour drive to my grandmother's house. Somehow we got it in our heads that we wanted to list all seven of the dwarves from Snow White. Every time we tried, we came up with six. We'd start over and come up with the same six names again. This was in the 1980s, so there was nowhere to look up this information, and even if there had been, we couldn't have done it from the interstate. Eventually, we gave up. We arrived at Mema's house, where she had our favorite spaghetti waiting for us. Five minutes later, with a mouthful of spaghetti, I yelled out "Bashful! It's Bashful!" Mema was confused, but we were happy (excited, not one of the other dwarves). It was one of the great "I got it!" moments of my childhood, and I sometimes advise kids today to stop themselves from looking things up now and then just so they could have moments like that too.

This phenomenon of figuring something out after you have stopped thinking about it feels mysterious, but it comes down to having two modes of thinking—one for the times when you are actively working on a problem or trying to remember something and another for when your mind is wandering in seemingly aimless ways. Barbara Oakley does a masterful job of explaining the mechanisms of our thinking and brain activity in *A Mind for Numbers*. She describes the activity in the brain's prefrontal cortex while your attention is actively on something as "focused mode." She states, "When you focus on something, the consciously attentive prefrontal cortex automatically sends out signals along neural pathways. These signals link different areas of your brain related to what you're thinking about." She describes it as "thinking tightly" because the neurons that link together something you are familiar with are likely near each other, and the thinking you are doing doesn't stray outside of that tightly connected loop. She says, "Your thoughts rattle easily through the previously ingrained patterns and quickly settle on a solution." This mode has obvious benefits, until you find yourself stuck. Then, the inability to veer away from the established route prevents you from finding the answer. It is then that you need to go into diffuse mode.

Think of focus mode as a workday and diffuse mode as a day off. On workdays, we mostly engage only with our coworkers, but we may run into an old friend in a coffee shop on our day off because we went somewhere other than work. While I was focused on the dwarves' names, I was stuck in a repeating neuron loop. Every time I searched that loop, I came up without the seventh dwarf. Bashful's name just wasn't in that particular set of neurons. He wasn't at work that day, so I couldn't find it there. When I was distracted by Mema's spaghetti, my brain was able to break out of that particular loop and find Bashful's name elsewhere. This is diffuse mode. Oakley describes diffuse mode by comparing it to a pinball machine where the bumpers are far apart from each other, allowing the pinball to travel farther and more freely. Because your thoughts are not caught in a tightly connected path, you are able to activate other neurons. This often happens when we are not focused on anything in particular, like while you are washing your hair or driving your car or just about to fall asleep. It's why you might have a sudden memory, insight, or creative idea during those times, the classic "aha moment."

In an article for Staying Ahead of the Game, author Evan Weinberger describes focused mode as "a bright light that shines directly on the most important information" while diffuse mode is akin to "a subtle, dim light that allows you to see a larger surface area." This visual is helpful in describing the benefits and drawbacks of each mode and why we need both. There are times when it is very important to pay close attention to one aspect of a concept in order to master it. If a biology student is going to describe what happens to the chromatids during mitosis, they must pay careful attention to each individual step. Once they have learned it well, the teacher could ask specifically about telophase, and they will be able to pull that information from a nice little package of known information. Other times, we need to see how content fits into the big picture. While it is good to know the role of the chloroplast during photosynthesis, it is important to recognize how it fits into the bigger picture of sugar production in its entire context. Timing makes a difference, too. You are more likely to be in diffuse mode when you are learning something new because there is not yet a well-established neuron pattern. Since you have that pattern after you have learned a skill, you are more likely to use focus mode when doing something you already know how to do.

One of the most effective tools for going into diffuse mode comes from an unexpected place—break time. We spend so much time telling ourselves and our students to focus that we often neglect the power of stepping away for a moment to regroup. We have all benefited from a quick stretch of our muscles or lap around the room, but we may not have understood why it was beneficial. It turns out that the benefit comes from spending a few seconds or minutes in diffuse mode. To some, taking diffuse mode breaks feels like a waste of valuable study time, but the reality is that it increases efficiency. After the break, you may return to a tricky problem to find that it wasn't as tricky as you thought. Your brain had worked on the solution behind your back.

During the acquisition of new content, there is an additional benefit to diffuse mode. Learning transfer takes time. If we keep cramming in new content without a break, we cause a traffic jam of information as the slower processing part of our brain tries to deal with the inflow. According to Barbara Oakley's 2019 Learning and the Brain session, switching from focus to diffuse mode allows the hippocampus and prefrontal cortex, those areas most involved with working memory, to get some relief as they have been overwhelmed during focused mode. Sending some of its content to the neocortex frees up space in the hippocampus for processing during the next focus session. Without the time in diffuse mode, there will be little transfer of new information to the long-term memory, much less the ability to connect the information with previously learned content, engage with it creatively, or extend it to other contexts. You have likely noticed this in your own life. When there are too many things going on at once, it is hard to attend to any one of them well.

Diffuse mode can be entered in a number of ways. You may have found this while untangling a difficult problem or figuring out how to answer an email. Sometimes, it may be as simple as taking a moment to close your eyes or look up at the ceiling. Other times, it may require a longer break. When I write recommendation letters, it can be hard to write on demand and fully capture the student in a concise way that will appeal to college admissions counselors. When I get stuck, I take a short walk around my neighborhood. The benefit may be partially due to increased blood flow and oxygen and sunlight, but it is likely also a function of spending time in diffuse mode. When I return to my computer, I locate the perfect phrase that I couldn't find before. Sometimes, sleep is beneficial. My parents were newly married while my dad was still in college, and my mom describes times when he would sit bolt upright in bed, spewing equations into the dark. He had gone to sleep with a difficult calculus problem in his mind, and the time he spent in diffuse mode, even while asleep, had allowed him to find solutions he couldn't while he was stuck in a focus loop. Time in diffuse mode, whether brief or extended, allows us to find something we wouldn't have if we had stayed in the tightly bound set of neurons that we use in focused mode.

Entering diffuse mode after a longer period of focused mode may be the best way to think creatively and develop novel ideas. In *Uncommon Sense Teaching*, Oakley and her colleagues say, "In focused mode, working memory is making connections among the neurons of the hippocampus and neocortex … In diffuse mode, working memory gets out of the picture and the brain subconsciously starts to make random connections." Since our brains are free to roam, neurons that normally don't spend a lot of time together have a chance for random encounters. Maybe, you make a connection between science and art that you hadn't before. Maybe something you learned in history is now giving you an insight into a piece of literature.

In the chapter on working memory, I described Mendeleev's method for externalizing what he knew about the elements, but there is more to that story. Due to a bout of insomnia as he worked on the pattern of elements, he stayed in focus mode for three days. Then, the story goes, he fell asleep during a snowstorm and had an extraordinary dream in which the elements fit together into a pattern he later developed into the periodic table. While the dream story is likely apocryphal, some time in diffuse mode followed his three day focused effort, allowing him to fit together the big picture of the chemical elements in a way he had not been able to while actively working on it. As teachers, we talk a lot about persevering through difficult times, and that is important, but we should also teach our students the value of stepping away for a moment in order to return with a refreshed hippocampus.

In the chapter on working memory, I mentioned taking time when students have reached cognitive load to take a brain break. This is not a novel idea. I hear teachers talk about brain breaks all of the time. Many teachers think there have to be full breaks where students leave the room to walk or play basketball, and thus, they devote too much class time to them. Sometimes, a full break is not needed. Just a moment in diffuse mode might give your hard working hippocampus a bit of relief. It can be as simple as taking a deep breath or closing our eyes to shut out visual stimuli. Most of us do that instinctively when we are trying to think of an elusive answer. A break in which we leave the room will involve more visual input, so it may not help as much as a few moments for students to simply close their eyes.

Eye closure for diffuse mode can even be helpful *during* your lesson. Most teachers believe that students pay better attention if they constantly keep their eyes on us, but it could be that having students close their eyes during a particularly challenging part of the lesson may prove helpful by reducing the distractions in their field of vision. I have had my students close their eyes when I wanted them to imagine something, but I had not considered before that they could benefit from closing their eyes while simply listening to me explain something complicated. Researchers Annelies Vredeveldt, Graham J. Hitch, and Alan D. Baddeley studied the effects of both visual and auditory distractions and their impact on recalling information. They found that participants who closed their eyes while receiving new information had better recall than those who experienced a visual distraction. They suggested that when people close their eyes, "it helps people to disengage from environmental stimulation and thereby enhance the efficiency of cognitive processing."

Much of the benefits our students get from diffuse mode will happen outside of our classrooms, while they do homework and study for tests, so we should teach them to take advantage of it. For decades, teachers have told students that cramming for tests doesn't work. Students don't believe that to be true because they can always point to a question they only got right because they studied it in the minutes just before the test. Since students care about grade performance, and teachers are focused on long-term learning, they are both kind of right. A student who has just seen a definition on a flashcard is likely to get it right when they see it on the test a few minutes later, but that is just recognition, not knowing. The teacher giving the advice understands that they won't remember it the next day or in the future because there hasn't been time for retrieval, rest, and then retrieval again.

When I was in high school biology, I was not exactly performing at my academic best, mostly because I sat next to my best friend, Kay, and behind a cute boy, named Chad. Kay, and I spent much of our class time trying to get Chad to turn around so we could smile at him. The academic content didn't have much of a chance of sticking. We decided in May that we should pull an all-nighter before the final exam and somehow got our parents to agree to this plan. We went to the corner store and bought hot cinnamon and sour lemon-flavored candies, reasoning that the sugar would give us energy and the spicy and sour nature of the candy would shock us into an alert state. (Keep in mind that we were sixteen, so our logic was a little weird.)

We gathered our school supplies and our sugar and tackled studying the entire biology textbook in one night. We focused hard and asked each other questions for three chapters. Then, because we thought the similarity of the words was hilarious, we put on Paula Abdul's "Vibeology" and danced our hearts out before sitting back down to study the next three chapters. When I tell this story to students, it is a warning against all-nighters. I make sure to tell them how falling asleep seventy-five questions into the exam made it difficult to perform well. I know what a bad idea this was, but there is one positive here. We accidentally discovered the value of rotating between focused and diffuse mode while studying. When we were busting a move and belting out "Oh, I love what you do when you do what you do," our brains were actually still actively processing the biology content we had learned in those three chapters in the background of our consciousness. We had unintentionally made up a modified version of the Pomodoro technique, alternating between focus and diffuse modes.

Personal trainers recommend alternating between upper body and lower body workouts every other day because of the time it takes the muscle fibers to reform after stressing them. In a similar way, mental rest is important between retrieval sessions because of the time it takes for myelination, a process I'll address more in Chapter 8, to increase the efficiency of neurons and for diffuse time. The cumulative effect of these sessions ultimately builds stronger mental connections. Since many of my students are athletes and artists, I return to the analogies of muscle building and play rehearsals frequently. No one trains for a marathon in one day; it requires a training process. No one memorizes a script in one night; actors know they need rehearsal time. We shouldn't expect something different from academic learning.

I love how Barbara Oakley sums this up perfectly in *A Mind for Numbers*. She says,

> The result of weeks and months of gradual effort? Sturdy neural structures with well-cured mortar laid between each new learning period. Learning this way, with regular periods of relaxation between times of focused attention, not only allows us to have more fun, but also allows us to learn more deeply. The relaxation periods provide time to gain perspective—to synthesize both the context and the big picture of what we are doing.

The breaks are not just breaks; they are consolidation periods that are critical to allowing what we have learned to become firm in our minds and connect with other learning. We aren't just stuffing knowledge into our heads indiscriminately; we are building interconnected schema networks. Without diffuse mode, schema building won't happen because we won't have allowed the brain time to reflect, grow, and interconnect.

In science classes, there are times when it is really important to remain in focused mode for a while. If your mind wanders while solving a Doppler effect, projectile, stoichiometry, or calorimetry problem, you are likely to misplace your variables and go astray without even realizing it. Losing focus in the lab has obvious dangers. Because of our need for them to remain in focused mode at certain times, it may be helpful to provide diffuse mode opportunities between challenging questions or train them to take advantage of it when they get stuck on a difficult problem.

In my physics class, for example, when we finish solving a combination circuit for the first time, I pause to ask if anyone is confused. They don't want to admit that they are, but a few brave souls will sometimes admit it. When I say, "Well, of course you are. This is the first time you have ever seen this. We are going to practice it for another day and a half," I can feel the relief from everyone in the room. They thought they were supposed to get it immediately, and being told they don't have to and that practice will make it easier is a gift. We do two circuits and then take a three-minute break before tackling the third. I do not give them homework that night because I want there to be ample spacing between learning to perform the process on the first day and practicing it on the next day. Their homework comes the second night. I have found that, for particularly complex material, gradual effort over multiple days has far greater benefit than intense effort in only one session.

Hannah Eichhorst teaches students about their bodies as part of her seventh-grade curriculum, so she has already taught them about the importance of oxygen and how breathing properly can influence other systems. When she notices that the class is in need of a moment to enter diffuse mode, she takes them through a deep breathing exercise and reminds them of the effects of breathing on their heart rate, blood pressure, and stress level. And just like that, she has taken advantage of diffuse mode and helped reinforce her content simultaneously. While no experiment has revealed an ideal length of brain break, my best advice is to make it the length of time you can afford in a given class period. You probably can't give up five minutes most days, but you probably do have time for them to stand up, do two jumping jacks, and sit back down.

I've recently been thinking about the concept of diffuse mode as doing something different with the brain rather than taking an actual break. In one of the weight lifting classes I take at the YMCA, we have a very long bicep-focused section. There are only so many ways to work the bicep, so there are a ton of curls with different rhythms and different grips, but they are still bicep curls. Twice during this section, we change to a bent-over curl, which our instructor, Matt calls an "active recovery." Even though it is still a curl and it is still working the bicep, it feels different. When we return to the next set of standing bicep curls, we feel as though we have had a little break, but we haven't wasted any workout time by just standing still. In a set with Joy, a different instructor, we do a combined set of bicep curls and tricep extensions. Moving back and forth between them allows rest for one part of the arm while working the other part. While I know the brain is not the same as a muscle, I have been wondering if a similar concept could apply. Could the concept of "active recovery" be something that I could use in my classroom? Perhaps taking a physical break isn't necessary to enter diffuse mode if I have my students focus on something else or change the manner in which we are thinking about the content. Is this why interleaving material works? I don't yet know the answer to these questions, but I think they are worth exploring. It is something I need to think about further and experiment with, but it feels like an appropriate way to take advantage of every precious minute of class time without overloading students in one area.

The time when our students need the benefits of diffuse mode the most is the time they are least likely to take advantage of it, during a test. When I pass out tests, I have often told students to remember that they can answer the questions in whatever order they want to. If they want to get the difficult questions out of the way while their minds are still fresh, that would be wise. However, most students don't do that as they are locked into the numbering system even when they know they don't have to be. After hearing Barbara Oakley speak about taking advantage of diffuse mode during testing by starting with the difficult problems and then taking a "break" when they get stuck by moving over to some easier questions before returning to the difficult ones, I have considered renumbering my tests, starting with the free response and ending with multiple choice. I haven't done it, but I think it is worth considering. I did start passing out the free response section first, and I think that has encouraged some of them to do those problems first because they don't want to wait to start. I'm not sure it has resulted in their shifting gears when they get stuck, but I'll take progress.

Hannah Eichhorst tells her students to put their head on the desk for a few seconds when they are stuck on a question, and she gives them the option of saying, "Can I pause this quiz?" When they "press pause," she hands them a children's book and lets them read a page or two before going back to the quiz. While this would be completely against my personality and would feel awkward in my classroom, it works in hers. Perhaps it would work in your classroom too.

Zane Smitley's biology tests are known to be difficult, but he also tries to help out the brains of his students as they take on the challenge of his tests. About halfway through the period, he has them cover the test with their reference sheet to take a thirty-second silent stretch break. When they sit back down, not only do they have more oxygen in their brains, but they reenter focused mode having cleared out some of the debris of the previous focus period.

I asked a few students to tell me how they take advantage of focus and diffuse mode while they are studying. Max, who you met in Chapter 2, told me that when he has a really hard test to study for, he goes to a casual restaurant at a low traffic time of day and spends a few hours studying. He cycles through different study methods, which he calls "read, write, restate, and recall" to give his brain some active recovery time during the focus periods. He said he would start with reading the material in the book, writing the information he thought was likely to be on the test, rewriting it in his own words, and answering the questions at the end of the chapter. Since he is at a restaurant, his breaks involve getting drink refills and visiting the restroom. While it would be impractical to do this with all of his tests, he has found this to be a workable method for those where he needs to spend significant time. I'm sure there are some for whom a restaurant would provide too much distraction, but Max felt the change of scenery and lack of access to the devices he had at home were helpful.

A high school junior, Kate, told me that she studies by "sandwiching" assignments. She does five calculus problems before switching to an AP history prompt. Then she does a few more problems before analyzing something for English. Her rationale for doing it is that she won't get hyper stressed over one thing and then have no energy for the others if she moves back and forth between them. She has implemented interleaving into her studies without even knowing what it is, and she is benefitting from it. While she is writing that history prompt, she is in diffuse mode about calculus. When she returns to calculus, she takes advantage of the background work her brain has been doing to help her strengthen her calculus skills.

When we give kids study advice, we can help them understand, as Max has, how a time of focus and diffuse modes will benefit them. We can talk about active recovery through task switching so that students like Kate can take advantage of it with more intentionality. We can communicate both to students and to their parents how studying with silent focus for twenty-five minutes followed by a five minute break to listen to music or watch an online video or have a snack aids their study in ways that two hours of constant work with earbuds playing music in their ears does not. Will they actually do it? Some will. The Kates and Maxes of the world want to do the things that will work best for them. And some won't because it is more comfortable to keep doing what they have always done, even if it isn't working for them. I do find it helpful to send the advice to parents after having taught it to students because some parents will help to reinforce the advice. Again, some will not because it isn't the way they did it. That's not up to us. We have to let go of whether or not they actually take advantage of our advice because we don't have control over their choices outside our classrooms. They don't like when I tell them to save their music for break times, but I show them the studies and say, "It's my job to tell you the truth. What you do with that truth is up to you, but you won't be able to say you didn't know." Give kids the best advice you can and leave the implementation to them.

5 Rich Encoding

I opened a physics class this way. "This is a picture of my cat, Max. When I first got him, I thought he would be bored in my apartment, so I bought a leash. Have you ever tried to walk a cat on a leash? It isn't so much taking him for a walk as taking him for a drag. I finally got him to the back side of the building, and there were two kids with a puppy. He broke the collar and ran up a tree. I was standing there with a collar dangling from a leash. After a lot of efforts to get him down, I did what every children's book has brainwashed me to do. What was it?" The students said, "You called the fire department." I said, "Yep, I called the fire department, and you know what? It's a myth, y'all. It's a lie. They do not come get your cat out of a tree, they do laugh at you on the telephone."

As I proceed with this story, my kids are hooked. It takes a lot longer to tell it than I have related above because I am pretty dramatic about dragging the cat around the building and go into more detail about my conversation with the fire department. But they are totally into the story with me. They are so interested in how I got the cat down from the tree that they don't even see me recording data to solve a problem about how gravitational potential energy is transformed into kinetic energy. By the end of the story, we are calculating the speed at which he hit the ground when my neighbor climbed the tree and dropped him out of it.

This story is a hook and a powerful connection to all the future calculations they will have to perform using the energy transformation concept. During a quiz, when a student calls me over to ask about a free fall problem, I just say, "That one is like that cat falling out of the tree," and they say, "Oh, okay." The story sticks with them and, if I have handled it well, guides them to a solid memory of the procedure.

According to Kathleen B. McDermott and Henry L. Roediger of Washington University, learning involves three interacting stages: encoding, storing, and retrieving content. The first step, encoding, involves the transfer of new information into long-term memory, and is at the heart of what we do as teachers. There are a lot of ways to do it. Rote encoding, the act of repeating a fact until it is remembered without regard to context, is sometimes necessary as with basic math facts or the order of the colors in the visible light spectrum, where there is no obvious deeper meaning to connect with. More often than not, however, it is better to engage in rich encoding activities for our students to give them deep understanding, provide relationships to other learning, and extend their knowledge beyond the classroom walls by connecting it to things they already know.

Why do rich encoding experiences help us remember content better than rote encoding? Psychologists have proposed a number of reasons, but for me, the most obvious is that we are likely to engage with material for a longer period of time when we are thinking about meaning than when we are simply repeating a list of seemingly unrelated facts for one simple reason—it is less boring. Another notion that intrigues me is that thinking about meaning is likely to involve more areas of the brain because we are connecting the meaning to sensory input, memories, and information we already know. Whatever the reason, we know that students will benefit from rich encoding whenever it is possible.

In every session John Almarode presents, he uses the term "learning experiences" rather than lesson plans. I like thinking of encoding in this way. It won't always be exciting, and I never promise fun. The learning experience may, in fact, sometimes be my direct delivery of new content, especially if it is something complex and in need of extensive explanation. It may sometimes be to drill with some flashcards in order to engage in retrieval. But thinking of it as an experience rather than a lesson broadens my thinking process, causing me to ask, "What is the student experiencing in his learning?" That propels me to find better activities, demonstrations, and metaphors to provide a richer learning experience for my students.

There are many ways to provide students with rich encoding experiences, especially in the science classroom. Some science teachers encode with carefully crafted lab activities or demonstrations. Some use problem-solving. Others like metaphors and stories. Perhaps you have your students create a collage interacting with what they are learning by putting them into categories, either on a physical poster or digital corkboard. They might process their learning through a short video or engage in a debate about a controversial scientific topic.

Rich Encoding Techniques
(Definitely NOT a complete list - add your own!)

Metaphor, Similes, and Analogies
Problem Solving
Story Structure
Using Language to Connect to Other Fields
Stimulating Curiosity with Mysteries
Demonstration and Lab Experiments

Figure 5.1 Rich encoding techniques.

I would posit that there is a place for all of these methods, depending on your content. Because metaphors work better with some concepts than others, there are times when it will be very useful and times when it will simply confuse the students. Some things lend themselves to debate in chemistry or environmental science while others do not, and there isn't time to debate everything. There often aren't resources to have a demonstration or lab with every concept we teach, so sometimes asking students to close their eyes and create a mental image may be the best way to proceed. Do what works where it works, but it is worth thinking about ways we can present our material in addition to straightforward telling. What we do is so varied, though, that straightforward telling is sometimes the best and most efficient method. Rather than going all in on one encoding method for everything, use your professional judgment to decide what works best in different situations. Think about the content you are delivering that day and what might be the best way to encode that particular information into the minds of your students.

Metaphors and Imagery

Metaphors are like mental coat hooks, something the student already has in place in their brain onto which they can hook their newly learned content. Why does it work? In his paper "On the Role of Analogies and Metaphors in Learning Science," Reinders Duit states, "Metaphors may open up new perspectives to us and may even help us to see the familiar in totally new ways" and that the act of comparing the content with the metaphor causes deeper thinking than the student might engage in without it. He asserts that this has a "generative power" as the student's brain must find the similarities between the metaphor and its object and that the surprising nature of a metaphor, relating it to something we previously hadn't, causes a reorganization of patterns in our brains. Kevin Washburn discusses how the metaphor takes advantage of additional mental pathways in encoding new information. He says, "Increasing the variety of ways the brain processes information increases connections between new and known information. Learners deepen their understanding of new information by representing it in varied forms."

Washburn suggests that there is additional power to representing the metaphor in nonverbal form, like drawings, because it requires depth of thought to make significant connections between the content and the representation. In a 2016 research study, Eliza Bobek and Barbara Tversky confirmed the concept. They asked students to create "visual explanations" of complex physical and chemical systems and compared their learning to those who used verbal-only explanations. The act of creating visual explanations helped all participants with understanding and remembering, but the effect was especially high in those who had tested low on spatial ability. The old aphorism about a picture being worth a thousand words may apply here. Since it is often easier to convey large amounts of information simultaneously with an image than with a lot of words, a vivid visual metaphor may be more helpful with encoding than lots of explanations. Using both visual and verbal systems provides richer encoding than either would alone. If the image can be animated to show a process, that's even better, and many topics can be found in animated form with a simple YouTube search.

Andy Tharby reminds us that "a metaphor or analogy provides a model of the truth, but not the truth itself." I tell my students that all analogies break down somewhere, so they should avoid trying to force everything about a concept into it. Otherwise, things get weird. It is one thing to use dating and breaking up as metaphors for synthesis and decomposition reactions, but it gets creepy if you try to keep using it for combustion reactions. It's okay to say, "We have reached the limit of this analogy." The point where it breaks down is a useful teaching moment. Knowing the ways in which a concept is different from something else is just as helpful with encoding as knowing the ways in which it is similar. I find the metaphors that work best are the ones I didn't have to work hard to think of. If I had to force it to fit, it probably won't be helpful to students in their thinking.

Imagery is usually easy in science. In chemistry, abstract concepts must be mentally pictured. "Imagine you are standing on a neutron in the nucleus of an atom. Look around. What do you see?" will give students a mental picture to connect to the Bohr models they are about to draw. In physics, making mental images of cars, sports, and dance makes the concept quite sticky. Biology teachers sometimes break processes like protein synthesis into movements, so students can imagine a moving image.

When Alyssa Powell teaches about concentration gradients, she has her students imagine that there are fifty students in the classroom and only three in the hallway and asks, "Where would you want to go?" This not only connects to a "real" experience, but it helps them imagine the process of osmosis. Zane Smitley spends a lot of time teaching photosynthesis, and students find the processes involved daunting. To help them understand the electron harvesting apparatus, he asks them to imagine that they are at a trampoline park, passing energy from one trampoline to another until they are high enough up to hold onto a suspended ball. Then, he asks them to imagine there is a zip line attached to the ball and compares it to the electron returning to lower levels as it gives off energy.

One word of caution: Metaphors are valuable because they are powerful, and sometimes they are more powerful than the concept itself, leading Mario Bunge to say "analogy may give birth to many monsters." In my class, for example, when I teach the dissolving of ionic compounds in water, I want students to understand that dissolving by dissociation is not decomposition. The ions have separated from each other, but the bonds have not been broken. I say,

> Imagine a married couple attending a party. They don't link arms and travel around as a unit, talking to people only as a couple. They separate and mingle, but they aren't divorced. When the party is over, the conditions that kept them apart no longer exist, so they go back home as a married couple. When an ionic compound, like salt, has dissolved in water, the sodium and chloride mingle with water molecules, but if you boil the water away, the water party ends, and the sodium and chlorine are still together.

It's a fantastic way to help them understand. What I have found, though, is that they tend to remember the metaphor alone. When I ask them to describe the process of dissociation on a test, they often start with, "It's like a married couple attending a party" and rarely mention the important parts of the actual dissolving process, like the poles of water molecules attracting the ions away from each other. They are encoding the wrong thing. Rather than abandon the metaphor, I combat wrong encoding by making sure to emphasize the chemistry in all retrieval opportunities, no longer referencing the metaphor.

Problem-Solving

Of course, metaphors are not the only way to encode new learning in a meaningful way. Humans are likely to think deeply about the meaning of a subject when using it to solve a problem. This may be what led to the popularity of problem-based learning approaches, although I believe those take the concept too far, asking students to go beyond their capabilities in frustrating ways. But solving kinematics problems in physics requires students to understand the relationships between changing velocity, rate of acceleration, distance, and time in a way that they wouldn't just by describing it in words. Early STEM education may build students problem-solving abilities, but they are unlikely to teach the concept upon which the problem is based. Employing explicit instruction in the concept before solving problems is the best way to prevent frustration in students while encoding the new learning through application. Physics and chemistry teachers have it easy in this area as most of our content lends itself to problem-solving, but some creative thinking will allow students to solve problems in biology and earth science as well. Ask students to think about how to produce the most ATP or how a geologist might go about analyzing rock layers that are buried beneath the ground. Again, I would say this works best if you haven't had to reach too far for a problem to solve. Think through the content you are teaching for a few minutes to see if there is a way to turn it into a problem, but if there isn't, choose a different encoding strategy.

Story Structure

In a June 2024 sermon, Rev. Jason Palacio said, "There is nothing more powerful than a good story. It can't be stopped." At first I thought this was a bit exaggerated, but after some reflection, I realized he was right. Stories capture and keep our attention in a way other delivery methods do not. When a friend tells me something as a fact, I listen for a shorter amount of time and remember less about what she has told me than I do when she tells me a story. In a story, I want to know what happens next, how the person in the story felt, and how the story ends. The same is true of fictional stories, which is why we pay attention for two hours or more in a movie theater.

Narrative stories are useful for maintaining attention and encoding new information as our brains appear to be uniquely wired to attend to and remember them. It seems that our brains process a story by perceiving the action in it in a way it doesn't with information presented in other ways. Perhaps because, before there was the written word, our ancestors passed down important information to their children orally, stories are assigned special status in human brains. Andy Tharby suggests that, in addition to being interesting and easy to understand, listening to a story also increases empathy. Therefore, we might be more likely to remember the information in it because it is more like a lived experience. Daniel Willingham has gone so far as to call the information from a story "psychologically privileged."

Not all material naturally lends itself well to a story, but it is worth scratching beyond the surface to find possibilities. In *Why Don't Students Like School*, Daniel Willingham acknowledges that not all information can be made into an actual story, but he encourages the use of story structure (Causality, Conflict, Complications, and Character) whenever possible in teaching new content. There may be ways to turn atoms, molecules, blood cells, or rock formations into characters with needs and obstacles to having those needs met, which leads to action. In science, it isn't hard to find cause and effect. Conflict and complications may just be other names for obstacles.

When talking about why something happens, it can be useful to assign motivation to the inanimate object at hand. When discussing the spontaneity of chemical processes, I call nature *lazy* because of its tendency to favor processes that result in lower enthalpy (energy) and *crazy* because of the preference for entropy (disorder). Then, I can say, "Okay, what does nature want? That's right. It wants to use less energy. What else does it want? It wants higher entropy. Okay, if this results in nature getting one of the things it wants, but not the other, what will happen?" The character is nature, and its desires are the cause of processes, but there may also be conflicts and complications in getting to the results. In earth sciences, you could ask students to imagine they are climbing through rock layers, riding on a lava flow, or rising through layers of the atmosphere. As they describe what they see in each layer, you can throw in other story elements to help them encode their understanding of what happens.

Personification and storytelling go hand in hand. In his TED talk, Tyler DeWitt, a middle school science teacher, describes how viruses work by introducing the character of a bacterium. When he says, "Don't get too attached to him," students are hooked. When he describes how the virus destroys the bacterium, students have an image they will not forget. The accurate picture in the textbook matters, but they'll forget it quickly if it is isolated. They won't forget it if they connect it to the story of the sick bacterium.

When I teach bonding, I personify the elements, imagining what they have, what they want, and what they might do to get what they want. "Have you ever been saving up to buy something? When you get really close to it, you'll babysit any kid or mow any lawn to get that last ten dollars, right? The atom is the same way. When it is close to an octet of valence electrons, it will bond with almost anything." This helps them understand why an element with seven valence electrons has higher electronegativity than those with four, and why the elements in families 1 and 17 are more reactive than the transition metals. The depth of science means information is often abstract and difficult to access intuitively. Giving students something more familiar to picture or relating it to common goals, motivations, and obstacles helps them connect to abstract ideas.

Connecting to Other Fields

The Latin origins of both the English language and scientific terms can be extremely helpful for encoding science instruction. I like breaking down scientific terms into their Latin roots and prefixes and then asking students for everyday words that contain those because it connects a new and potentially intimidating vocabulary word to something they have an experience with in other areas of their lives. Connecting to words whose roots students already know activates prior knowledge and builds schema as we talked about in Chapter 3, but it also requires them to think about meaning.

When I learned that the prefix *micro-* means "small," the prefix *tele-* means "far," and the root word *scope* means "to see," I was given the tools to decode any word that included those parts. When I encountered words like microscope and telescope and endoscope and television and telephone and microchip, I could mix and match those parts. That came in handy on the SAT because it helped me to eliminate wrong answers, but it has also been essential as a science teacher because most of our terms have Latin or Greek origins. Learning English vocabulary this way helped me encode what I was learning in biology, chemistry, anatomy, math, and physics. Once I learned that the suffix *-itis* means "inflamed" or "infected," I had some understanding of medical terms that include that suffix, from the common ones like *tonsillitis* and *appendicitis* to more challenging ones like *endocarditis* (which I can deduce has something to do with the inflammation of something inside the heart because I was also taught the meanings of *cardio* and *endo-*). That stuck with me, so in the science classes that I teach, I break down words like atom, heterogeneous, transparent, and rectilinear and make connections to the word parts to whatever words I think they may already know. The word atom is made of *a*, which means "not" (as in atheist or anonymous), and *tom*, which means "to cut" (like appendectomy or tonsillectomy). This helps students to understand that Democritus thought of the atom as something that could not be divided. The prefix *trans-* means "across," so I have them connect transparent and translucent with words like transport and transfer, which are easily accessible as taking something across a space. The prefix *rect-* in rectilinear means "straight," and while that word sounds complex, they already know words like "direct" and "rectangle," so I make sure to connect to those. Knowing that makes the term *rectilinear propagation* (straight line travel of waves) easier to understand and remember. After years of relating the word propagation to propaganda, a student augmented my explanation by bringing up the propagation of plants, making the encoding richer than it had been before.

There's nothing quite like having the student make the connection for you. For many years, I have taught that the word circuit comes from the same root as circle, implying that the electricity returns to where it started, but they got a little hung up on thinking that circuits had to be circular in shape. This year, an eighth grader said, "like circulation," and I wished I had thought of that two decades ago. It's a much better connection and can be easily pictured with moving blood cells as an analogy to moving electrons.

Connecting scientific information to other fields will help your students who think they don't like science. When they realize these weird sounding terms come from the same roots as terms in dance, art, sports, and other things they like, they will find the terms less intimidating. It gives them a chance to add their own expertise to the discussion, and it makes the information stickier because it doesn't feel disconnected from the other parts of their life. If you want to do this but don't know how, add the word "etymology" to a Google search for a word. It will tell you the word's history and the meaning of each part.

Stimulating Curiosity

In the introduction, I talked about how many questions young children ask. They do so with no end objective other than finding the answer. Somewhere in early middle school years, some well-meaning adult introduces the idea that they should only learn what they "will use later in life." They come to view education merely as job training and lose the joy of learning for its own sake. Our response to that shouldn't be reducing rigor or letting them dictate what they learn. It should be to reintroduce them to the joy they once found in learning. We should start by modeling that in our own lives. Talk about the books you read and the podcasts you listen to. Tell them what you are wondering about. Did you recently learn something that excites you? Share that excitement with them as you tell them about your new knowledge. Seeing adult role models as lifelong learners is powerful for students who have become jaded.

Curiosity is stimulated by unanswered questions. In his book *Uprise*, Kevin Washburn extols curiosity as a part of the learning mindset. He says, "The brain does not like unanswered questions. It will keep pursuing answers even when you are not conscious—hence the 2:30 solution to a problem you've recently encountered." When we ask students interesting questions or share ours with them, we can create the curiosity necessary to motivate finding answers.

Students are used to answering with some of the right words and being affirmed for "being on the right track." It may take time to break students of that habit in order to get them to think curiously, but it is possible if we persevere. I ask my physics students why we can see through the window but not the door. They start with the most obvious, surface-level answer—"because one is made of glass and the other of wood." I reply, "Okay, but the question I'm asking is why we can see through glass and not wood." Their reply is just to reword the question I asked them as an answer, saying, "Because glass is transparent and wood is not." I am experienced with this conversation, so I am undaunted. "Way to say some science words, guys. But the question I'm asking is what causes that to be true. Science is about finding out why something happens the way it does." I eventually relieve the tension by telling them that I know they don't know this fairly complex answer. Then, I show them a great TED video that illustrates the answer better than I can explain it using only words. While it would save time if I said, "Today, I want you to learn why we can see through some things and not others. Here's a TED video that explains it," I choose to spend time getting them to ask the next question because I want to make them more curious people, a quality that will have lasting effects outside of my lesson.

In Chapter 2, I mentioned that I post my learning objectives as questions rather than statements. Instead of writing, "Objective: To calculate change in pitch using the Doppler Effect," I write, "Objective Question: How does movement influence the pitch of a sound?" I do this because I believe students might have their curiosity stimulated by the question rather than simply being told what we are going to do. I have performed no experiments to see if this is effective, but since it takes the same amount of time to write a question as it does to write a statement, I see no negative side.

Demonstrations and Labs

As a science teacher, I love good demonstrations. They are less time-consuming than labs, require fewer resources, and are often more likely to work properly. Approached correctly, they are powerful tools for encoding new learning and aiding memory. Done poorly, they have little more than entertainment value.

So, how can a demonstration be done well to optimize learning? The first thing to consider is whether to demonstrate before or after the learning. I suggest that most of the time, the answer is after. But, it's not always the case. If there is a mystery to be solved that the kids can solve with some guiding questions from you, it might be best to do the demonstration before the lesson as it will stimulate curiosity. If I can put a question in their minds using a demonstration, I definitely will.

For example, when I teach Bernoulli's Principle, I start my class by placing a sheet of paper on top of two books. I bring a student to the front of the room and ask the class what they think will happen if they blow air into the gap beneath the paper. Understandably, all students believe the paper will fly up. I have the student blow under it and amaze everyone when the paper is pulled down instead of up. When asked to explain why, students throw out a lot of interesting guesses, but they cannot arrive at the answer without help. I ask guiding questions about what is happening with the air molecules, drawing illustrations on the board, and I eventually lead them to a basic understanding of why pressure is lower when a fluid is moving. We then go to the book and look at the actual statement of Bernoulli's Principle, and I walk them through diverse examples of the same concept, from the flight of airplanes to curve balls to the effects of a tornado on a house to the odd behavior of shower curtains when they move in on you. Because students can make the connection with a little support and some guiding questions, I find it helpful to pique their curiosity with that demonstration before learning the concept.

If, however, the concept is particularly complex, it is probably better to demonstrate it after explicitly teaching the concept. Alyssa Powell told me, "I do it after explicit instruction because they just don't have the foundation they need to make the connections without my teaching it first."

I teach two gas laws, Charles's Law and Boyle's Law, to eighth-grade physical science students. Because they have no foundation at all, I teach Charles's Law one day and demonstrate it with that lesson. I teach Boyle's Law the next day and then demonstrate it. Then, after having learned both concepts, we tackle the math on day three. The chemistry teacher Melanie Dunning takes a different approach than what I do, because her students are older. She teaches all of the gas laws and the math for several days. At the end of the unit, they go into the lab where there are stations with each gas law represented in an experiment. The students perform the experiment as described in the instructions, and it is their job to predict what will happen and explain which law it is showing. She does something similar with predicting the results of a reaction, and that also can only be done after explicitly teaching what happens in single and double replacement reactions. Otherwise, they aren't predictions as much as wild guesses.

As you can see, there are many ways to provide rich encoding experiences for teaching students meaningful information, and this is by no means a complete list. I haven't mentioned technology as a method because it can be used as a vehicle for any method. Daisy Christodoulou wrote, "Don't start by thinking about the technology. Start by thinking about the problem you have, and then thinking about how technology can solve it." I would recommend that you apply this line of thinking to all pedagogy. Keep the learning at the forefront of your mind. Then choose your methods based on what you want them to learn and do with that learning. Sit down with your content and give it some thought. Would this content lend itself well to story structure or problem-solving? Are there ways to bring in my students who are more inclined to the humanities by referencing a play or song or by showing a connection between terms in different contexts? Would a demonstration of this concept make it clearer? Return again to the idea of learning experiences. What are students experiencing in this class that will help them to learn this content?

6 Getting the Most from Discovery Learning

Engagement Is a Means, Not an End

Years ago, I wrote a review song for my eighth-grade students to use as they study for their midterm exam. The chemistry content is set to tunes of TV theme songs like *The Flintstones* and *Gilligan's Island*. I like to hand out the lyrics in the form of a songbook, but I don't know how to make booklets on the school copier. When I ask office staff to teach me, they generally make the books for me. That's a lovely gesture, and I am grateful they are willing to do it, but I really want to learn how to do it myself. It's a busy time of the year and people find it less time-consuming just to do it for me, so no one has explicitly taught me how to do it yet.

Two years ago, I decided to figure it out myself one morning when no one else was at school. For forty minutes, I tried a number of things that proved unsuccessful. Then, I Googled how to make booklets, but the initial search results used programs and copy machines that didn't match mine. At one point, I thought I had found it, but when I looked at my computer, I didn't have the buttons shown in the instructions. I finally realized the instructions were for documents in Adobe Reader while I was in Preview, which is not the same thing. When I got the document open in Reader, I found the right buttons, but the printed result was missing two pages and inexplicably ended on the third page of the original rather than the eighth page. I kept trying things and changing settings until it finally came out right and made the eighty-one copies I needed.

Supporters of discovery learning, I hear you saying, "See—you were motivated, active in your learning, used your tools, and you will remember it longer than if someone had just told you how to do it." Here's the thing, though. I don't remember how to do it. Someone asked me the next week how to make a booklet, and I could not tell them. I had spent quite a lot of time, paper, ink, and energy for learning that had no permanence. If I tried to do it today, I could save a little of that time by starting with Google and remembering to open it in Reader rather than Preview, but I would still be floundering around through instructions that didn't quite work and throwing away a lot of paper from failed trials. If someone had explicitly taught me the steps and given me feedback while I did it, I would likely have learned it well and be able to do it now.

Like many educational terms, "Discovery Learning" (or Inquiry Learning, Minimally Guided Instruction, Challenge Based Learning, Project Based Learning—I know they are not all the same, but most people use them interchangeably) is loaded with baggage, so we need to understand what we mean by it. According to Paul Kirschner, Richard Clark, and John Sweller, "Minimally guided instruction is when teachers offer partial or minimal guidance so that learners are expected to discover some or all of the concepts and skills they are supposed to learn on their own." The *Oxford Reference* online dictionary gives this definition:

> Discovery learning is an approach to learning in which the learner is allowed to explore and become actively engaged with concepts, objects, or the physical environment in order to develop their understanding of it. In this process, the teacher is a facilitator rather than an instructor, and it is their role to organize a rich or appropriately resourced learning environment and to encourage the learner's self-directed curiosity and problem-solving skills, rather than to demonstrate or provide "correct" answers.

Promoters and detractors each focus on whichever aspect confirms our biases. Advocates of discovery learning focus on the phrase "actively engaged" because everyone wants that for their students. Skeptics, like me, focus on phrases like "facilitator rather than instructor" and "rather than to demonstrate or provide correct answers" because our concern is that students with only minimal guidance will not encode things properly.

The book *How Learning Happens* by Kirschner and Hendrick includes the article "Why Discovery Learning Is a Bad Way to Discover Things / Why Inquiry Learning Isn't." In it, they assert that "the instructional practices involved in Discovery Learning ignore the structures that constitute human cognitive architecture" and are "not likely to be effective or efficient." Their primary explanation is working memory overload. The student is using all of the facilities of their working memory to search for information and problem-solving and there is no space for the creation of long-term memory formation.

One method of discovery learning is to have students engage in an activity and then ask them three questions: (1) What did you notice? (2) What do you wonder? (3) What conclusions can you draw? This approach appeals to people because it seems like an engaging and inspiring way to learn. We forget that this is the method that was used for millennia before Galileo. Observation, wondering, and drawing conclusions gave us the theory of the four humors and the idea that the Sun revolved around the Earth. I'm not being critical of them because they didn't know a better way. We do. We are the beneficiaries of seven centuries of the scientific method, with each generation building on the discoveries of the ones before. I was a student in a university class that used *Discovering Calculus*, and I remember saying, "There's a reason it took from the beginning of time until Isaac Newton to discover calculus; how am I supposed to do it in a semester as a college freshman?"

Those who believe strongly in discovery learning methods will often admit that it is a messy process but say that it will teach students to "think like scientists." It's an enchanting idea, but scientists were novices first. They didn't and couldn't jump straight to expert level thinking without a foundation. There are a lot of science teachers who are made to feel guilty if they are not in the lab every day. Perhaps you are one of those teachers, dealing with the pressure from administration and parents. Perhaps you have been told that you shouldn't teach things explicitly but allow students to discover science principles for themselves. Yet, you know when you take your students in the lab without any explicit instruction, they don't leave with the knowledge you want them to. If that describes you, please take solace in this statement from Stanislas Dehaene's book *How We Learn*. It made me sit up straighter, grip my highlighter, and tear up a bit. "The fundamentally correct view that children must be attentively and actively engaged in their own learning must not be confused with classical constructivism or discovery learning methods—which are seductive ideas whose ineffectiveness has, unfortunately, been repeatedly demonstrated."

Daniel Willingham is generous with discovery learning while also warning readers to use it with care. In his mind, the positive is that if students have a voice in deciding, they will be more actively engaged with the material and be more likely to think about it deeply. It is important to remember, however, that engagement is a means, not an end. While unengaged students cannot learn, a room full of engaged students is not, by itself, an indication that learning is happening. As Willingham points out, we cannot predict what students will think about when they are constructing their own learning. He says, "If students are left to explore ideas on their own, they may well explore mental paths that are not profitable. If memory is the residue of thought, then students will remember incorrect discoveries as much as they will remember correct ones." Don't be fooled by engagement alone. Students would be engaged if I showed them the latest superhero movie, but they are learning my curriculum. Willingham's advice is to design assignments in such a way that thinking about the meaning of the content is unavoidable. We must carefully think about that during the planning of lessons. Barbara Oakley and her colleagues recommend timing discovery-based experiences as a reinforcement after concept mastery, saying, "Discovery-based learning can be useful after difficult concepts and skills are mastered. But when it comes to introducing more difficult material without careful teacher guidance, students can become lost in the forest."

I am not saying that we shouldn't have lab experiences, demonstrations, manipulatives, or projects. Those things are valuable and can help with rich encoding as I described in the last chapter. What I am saying is that the experiment alone is not a teacher. Guidance is needed to give students a foundation on which to build and the tools to build with. In their article "Putting Students on the Path to Learning," Kirschner, Clark, and Sweller put it in strong terms, saying, "The past half century of empirical research has provided overwhelming and unambiguous evidence that, for everyone but experts, partial guidance during instruction is significantly less effective and efficient than full guidance."

Given the amount of time they take, I choose my lab experiments very carefully. I choose the ones that I can explicitly prepare students for, that can be carried out without much technical difficulty or chance of failure, that I can meaningfully follow up on to ensure they have learned what I want them to, and that I can refer back to in future chapters. Otherwise, it is just activity for the sake of appearing engaged.

It's important to note that no one expects children to learn by discovery in other structured learning environments. A basketball coach explicitly teaches his players how to properly shoot a free throw, assesses their performance while they practice it multiple times, and provides feedback. He does not hand them a ball and say, "Use your resources to figure out what a free throw is, when you might use it, and how to do it." Personal trainers don't encourage their clients to figure out a form that works for them, knowing it would result in injury if they did. Instead, they show their client the proper form and then stand by and provide feedback while it is performed. An apprentice mechanic is not encouraged to destroy a car so that he can learn about it by discovery; he is carefully taught and monitored by a mentor. Students of cosmetology are first taught principles and then practice on wigs before being allowed to apply a pair of scissors to the hair of a human client; and even then, they are closely watched by an instructor and provided with feedback throughout the process. In all other areas of our lives, we seem to understand that for a person to learn something new, they need to be taught. It is only in school that we have convinced ourselves that novice learners are capable of thinking like experts without the guidance of an expert.

One of the primary arguments in favor of discovery learning is that students will less likely be bored and more likely to have a positive attitude about their learning. Researchers R. Russell Wilke and William J. Straits decided to investigate this in an introductory biology course. The results are mostly good for those who back the discovery method as they found students' attitudes were generally positive in surveys, and content was well-remembered on a subsequent end of semester exam. The news is less positive if your goal in discovery learning is to get students to "think like scientists" as their lowest scores on the exam came from questions related to experimental design. It is also important to note, I think, that the class was not structured with an entirely inquiry-based approach. There were four discovery activities during a semester of direct instruction from an expert teacher. Used in combination, the more active approach enhances direct instruction. While praising a discovery pedagogy in the paper, they still seem to understand it would be a poor way to structure an entire course. The conclusion states, "The limited use of discovery learning in combination with more traditional practices can improve students' achievement." If you are going to use it, do so judiciously.

Much of your success or failure with a discovery approach will come down to what you are trying to teach with it. If you are teaching students about something simple, intuitive, and well-defined, like acceleration caused by gravity, it may work because it will be easy for them to design an experiment around it. If it is especially complex, like what causes glass to be transparent while other materials are not, it is likely to confuse rather than enlighten because it will be difficult to draw the conclusions needed from something so deeply buried beneath the surface. They are not going to arrive at a quantum mechanics–based conclusion themselves.

Let me go back to Dr. Dehaene for a moment. A paragraph after the sentence that stopped me in my tracks, he said, "When children are left to themselves, they have great difficulty discovering the abstract rules that govern a domain, and they learn much less, if anything at all. Should we be surprised by this? How could we imagine that children would rediscover, in a few hours and without any guidance, what humanity took centuries to discern?" I took a moment to congratulate my college self and then mulled over the phrase "abstract rules." That is exactly why constructivism doesn't work. They can observe the experiment, which has value; but they have no idea of why the experiment works because the concepts are too abstract. So, in a science class, where our job is to teach why things happen, we are seduced by the idea that they will figure it out if we merely show them what happens. It doesn't teach them to "think scientifically," which is the well-meaning idea behind inquiry-based learning because the deep structure is not yet available to them. We are naturally curious, but we are not naturally scientists. That is why it took from the beginning of time until Galileo to think of experimentation in spite of really smart philosophers observing and hypothesizing about the natural world. Why would we want students to return to inefficient and ineffective methods of the past, hoping they will develop scientific thought processes anew, when they can stand, as Isaac Newton said, "on the shoulders of giants"?

Allow me to illustrate this with the story of my most epic classroom failure. In the early 2010s, I had bought into the idea of students learning more from struggling to solve a problem than by having me tell them. I had a project at the time that involved electricity, so I thought it would be a good idea to replace it with a challenge-based learning project. At this time, my physics class had only nine students who were usually game for trying new things. I was friends with a former missionary to Haiti where they had electricity rationing, so I brought him in to share his story about living in a place with inconsistent access to electricity, stopping the story just before the part where he solved the problem. He shared why it was really important for a family to keep their refrigerator running to avoid food spoilage and to keep fans running to blow off disease-carrying insects. He left, and I set them the challenge. "How would you ensure a consistent supply of electricity to your home when the city you live in doesn't supply it?"

To be honest, I didn't think this would be a very difficult challenge for them as either generators or solar panels would be fairly reasonable solutions. The most charitable description I have for their brainstorming session was that it was interesting. By interesting, I mean bizarrely entertaining. They suggested stealing electricity from the Dominican Republic and Cuba as well as harnessing the power of electric eels. I've been teaching long enough to know that students sometimes throw silly ideas out at the beginning of brainstorming sessions for fun before getting down to real work, so I didn't worry much about it that day. Then I began hearing from other teachers. One of them said that a physics student had come to her, distressed that Miss Hawks was trying to get them to "solve the energy crisis." Clearly, something had been miscommunicated, so I sent an email clarifying what we were actually trying to do, not solve a problem for the world, the country of Haiti, or even a town, just their own home.

They had one day per week to work on this for seven weeks, so I looked forward to progress being made. For the first two weeks, it was silent in my room. I don't mean it was kind of quiet. I mean it was graveyard-quiet. These were nine people who were supposed to be collaborating. At the end of the second week, I asked them about it. "You want us to talk in class?" was their response. I told them that most people, when given a project workday, did talk about what they were doing. It got slightly better. I started hearing some murmurings about something with a lawn mower motor, which I considered progress—until the following Wednesday. One of my students showed up with a bag full of lemons and a pile of wires. He sat at the table, stripping the insulation off of the wires. When asked what he was doing, he said, "stripping wires." Some of the others were baffled because they had a plan with a lawn mower motor that had nothing to do with lemons. This was not going well, but I was committed to the idea that I wasn't supposed to be guiding them, so I asked questions, but I did not give them any ideas. On the last day of the project, one of them had attached a 2-inch solar panel to the world's smallest fan. Another brought in a handheld steam generator, which lit a 10 W light bulb. Needless to say, there had been little discovery or learning in this experience, and I didn't know how to begin assigning a grade to the fiasco. I have modified this into a great project over the years, but it has a lot more parameters and direct instruction now than it did at the start. Never again will I engage students in a purely unguided experience.

In *The Great Divorce*, C. S. Lewis wrote, "Thirst was made for water, inquiry for truth." If our students inquire, but it ends there, what was the purpose?

Many of our colleagues would say the value lies in the fact that they did it themselves. But if the end goal is to find truth, to get answers, then a student led inquiry that doesn't lead to answers has little worth. It is as absurd as a thirsty man in the desert being proud to find a few drops of dew on his own when a guide who was familiar with the area could have led him to a nearby freshwater spring. As educators, we know the land. We know where the springs of knowledge are and have the skills to lead our students to them. Why would we withhold that from them? Why would we watch them search on their own to find something less valuable?

As I mentioned earlier, I choose my labs carefully, which means I do fewer of them than some people would like to see. To properly learn from a lab experience, a lot of time must be spent in both preparation and follow-up. If you skip the preparation, most of them won't know what they are meant to observe while performing in the lab. It may seem obvious to you what they are meant to notice, but I assure you that it will not be obvious to them. If you skip the follow-up, they will usually leave with quite a few wrong conclusions. As John Dewey is credited with saying that if we want to learn from an experience, we must also reflect on it. It is also important that our reflections be aided by guidance from a knowledgeable helper. As a teacher, I know which follow-up questions will help them arrive at the right conclusions; they don't know what questions to ask themselves to make that happen. In all of my interviews with science teachers, only one, Hannah Eichhorst, advocated for discovery learning. She does a lot of student exploration without explicitly preparing them ahead of time. I have, however, observed her many times. She engages students in guided inquiry, and she does a lot of explicit instruction as she circulates the room, answering their questions and explaining the concepts. She just does it in small groups rather than full class style.

At the end of the bonding chapter in physical science, I have students separate salt into sodium and chlorine by running an electrical current through salt water. This is at the end of the chapter, so I have taught them about the difference between ionic and covalent bonds, using salt as a frequent example of an ionic bond. I have taught them what ions are and why they function as electrolytes in aqueous solutions. Before we enter the lab, I remind them of those features of ionic bonds. During the class period, while they answer some observation questions on the front side of the page, I circulate from table to table, going over the questions from the back of the page with each group.

I start with the question, "What elements are in salt?" They usually get that one right. I then ask what they think is in the bubbles they see coming off of one of the wires. First, they answer "electricity" or "smoke," so I remind them that bubbles are always filled with gas. Then they answer "carbon dioxide" because it is the only gas some of them know. I remind them that I asked question one for a reason, so we can get to the correct answer of chlorine. Then, I ask them what the metal buildup on the other wire is. You might think they would realize it is the other element in salt, but they once again revert to the metals they commonly hear about, copper and iron. I again remind them that what they have done is split the salt into sodium and chlorine so that we can get to the correct conclusion. The fourth question is about why salt water conducts electricity, and most of them answer something like "because sodium is a metal and metals conduct electricity," so we have a follow-up conversation after the lab experience about electrolytes.

As you can see, there is a fair amount of explicit instruction before, during, and after the lab experience. If you aren't willing to invest that kind of time, students are not going to get what they should from the lab. They will not learn what you intend for them to learn just by performing the experiment. Mine would come away thinking there was smoke coming from one wire and copper on the other and that this all happened because the sodium metal in salt carries electricity, none of which is accurate. Worse yet, they would leave falsely believing they had learned the concept well because they "saw it with their own eyes." As Dr. Dehaene says, "Perhaps the worst effect of discovery learning is that it leaves students under the illusion that they have mastered a certain topic without ever giving them the means to access the deeper concepts of a discipline." My best advice is that after any lab experience, whether guided or inquiry-based, you follow up extensively to identify and address the misinterpretations that have almost certainly happened.

Because of the time it takes, make sure the lab experiments you choose reveal important topics that can be referenced more than once. The electrolysis of salt lab is in my lesson plan because, not only does it help them understand ionic bonds, I also refer to it multiple times during the semester in reference to endothermic reactions, decomposition, and dissociation. Even in the second semester, when we have moved from chemistry to physics, I occasionally find myself referencing this experiment.

If you do decide that you want to engage in some discovery learning, make sure to keep the content front and center. I appreciate this word of caution from Barbara Oakley and her coauthors in *Uncommon Sense Teaching* when they address student-directed forms of encoding. They say, "Planning effective student-directed learning activities isn't for the faint of heart. Such instruction requires significant prep work. Be careful not to be seduced by 'Pinterest planning'—that is using arts and crafts as an extension activity." Keep the content front and center and have your goals clear in the minds of both your students and yourself. Otherwise, you will be inclined to believe that students have learned something just because they were engaged in making a product that looks pretty. They advise continuously circling back to the standards and objectives of your lesson to make sure it lines up with what you are having your students do, creating the clarity we addressed in Chapter 2.

No one tries to stray away from student learning, but it happens when we mistake engagement for learning. Discovery learning is a seductive idea, and you probably will experience pressure from people who do not understand its limitations. Stick to what you know is true, and do what is best for your students. Whether you decide to use it or not, recognizing its limitations will help you to navigate the challenges of its use or defend its nonuse in the best ways possible.

7 Modeling and Scaffolding

One of the most difficult chapters in my eighth-grade physical science class is the one about chemical bonds. When we learn to write chemical formulas and name compounds for binary ionic, binary covalent, and polyatomic ionic bonds, there is a lot to remember as the rules are different for each type. For several years, when students came in for help, I drew a chart on paper, comparing and contrasting the rules for each type and showing examples and exceptions. I handed it to them at the end of our discussion, and they left to study with it. When another student came on a different day, I drew the chart again. I repeated this process with students in help classes for two years before I realized I should make a copy of the chart. It took another two years before I recognized it might help everyone, digitized it, and started posting it on our learning management system at the beginning of the unit.

I had modeled the process of each skill during the class and had given them time to practice each individually, but the difficulty came when they were interleaved. The chart served as a scaffold to help them identify the bond type and apply the rules for each. During class time, I was encoding the knowledge that I hoped would make the scaffold obsolete by asking questions like, "What type of bond have I written on the board? Yes, it is covalent. How can you tell? What prefix do I use for five? How do we change the ending since it ends in a non-metal?" The hope was that all of this modeling and practicing and retrieving would make the chart dispensable as it would now be in their minds.

Modeling is exactly what it sounds like—providing an example of an ideal answer or product. The teacher shows students how to solve a problem, construct a graph, write a hypothesis, construct a data table, and so on. Teachers can perform live-modeling, where students watch the teacher perform the entire process step-by-step in front of them with narration. We can also provide completely worked-out examples, so students see the entire product before interacting with the process themselves. I'm a fan of both, starting with live-modeling and then pointing them to a resource with a worked-out model to refer to during independent practice. It's not hard to understand why this is an important part of teaching. It gives students success criteria, which is important for the clarity we addressed in Chapter 2, and it prevents them from unknowingly going down wrong paths. You probably never had to be told to model because it is such an obvious practice.

Yet, in my early career, I was a bit concerned about providing detailed models. This was more true with projects than daily work, but I worried that the students would just copy my example. This concern may have been the result of a cultural attitude that sees copying someone else as less important than original thought. Perhaps my thoughts were influenced by concerns that my students wouldn't be engaged. I have, however, since learned the value of mimicry in the early stages of learning and no longer have such objections to providing detailed models. This cultural resistance seems to be a modern phenomenon. Historically, mentors in fields from art to medicine taught their apprentices to copy them for a while so that they could understand the fundamentals of their disciplines before allowing them to include individual variations. Even in the New Testament book of Luke, Jesus says that a student, "when fully trained, will be like his teacher." First-century schoolmaster, Quintillian, encouraged copying first. He said, "It is from these and other authors worthy of our study that we must draw our stock of words, the variety of our figures and our methods of composition, while we must form our minds on the model of every excellence. For there can be no doubt that in art no small portion of our task lies in imitation." In his journal article "The Theory and Practice of Imitation in Classical Rhetoric," Edward Corbett explained that the ancient Greek and Roman philosophers and teachers actively encouraged imitation in order to master details of thinking processes. They considered high-quality imitation to be a rigorous activity, including memorization of a text, reciting it fully, and only then transforming it through paraphrasing or turning it into poetry. It is clear that they believed modeling preceded creativity. Providing models to our novice learners is not only acceptable, it is necessary for getting them to the next level of learning. According to John Almarode and Kara Vandas, modeling is part of clarity and helps to instill confidence in students as they learn.

Scaffolding is a more difficult challenge. It is less well-implemented, if ever implemented at all. First, let's talk about what it is and what it isn't. According to Nancy Boblett, in her paper "Scaffolding: Defining the Metaphor," Scaffolding describes "a system of temporary guidance offered to the learner and then removed when the learner no longer needs it." It is a model, but it is not doing the thinking for them. It is a support, but it is not a permanent one. Mary Bigelow describes scaffolding as "guiding strategies designed to help students develop greater understanding of concepts and skills to become more independent learners." I like this description because of its emphasis on leading them to independence. Any parent who has taught his child to ride a bike knows he will not hold onto the seat and run alongside the young rider forever, but he also knows he has to wait until the child has a sense of balance on two wheels before he can let go. The same is true in educational scaffolds as they help students get a sense of the task before being asked to do it without aid. Scaffolding can take a variety of forms, but no matter what it looks like, there are usually two features. It provides support to students as they learn, and it is removed after they gain proficiency.

A scaffold is temporary. If it is never removed, it is not a scaffold. It should not, however, be removed the day before an assessment because students need a chance to practice without it. I took a lesson from our theater teacher, Jaime Hartley, when I attended a play rehearsal on a day the cast calls "Crash and Burn Day." Up until that day, actors have been allowed to hold their scripts on stage and consult them when needed. There reaches a time, however, when they cannot develop any further with movement, blocking, and character development if they are not "off-book." That first off-book rehearsal is, as you might imagine, an absolute disaster—hence the name. If that were the day before the performance, it would be a catastrophe of epic proportions. They need quite a few rehearsals off-book before they are ready to perform for an audience. The same is true of scaffolds in learning. Students must know when the scaffold will be removed and what they should be able to do by that date, or it will feel cruel when you remove it, and it must be far enough ahead of the test that they have a chance to practice the number of times required to rebuild their confidence without it.

In the cardio kickboxing class I take at the YMCA, my instructor, Matt, teaches several individual sequences and has us perform them eight to sixteen times before putting them into combinations and then reducing the number of reps of each part in the combination. As we get more fluid from week to week, he speeds up the process. We can do the same with academic skills in science classes. We can ask students to complete tasks with increasingly less input from us until they are ready to take it on themselves.

As with modeling, I was hesitant in the early years of my career to provide scaffolds, but that is because I didn't understand how to properly implement them. I thought they would prevent students from performing tasks without "the crutch." What I have since learned is that they can be valuable in the early part of learning a new skill. Yet, I am not the only one to find it challenging to include in my classes. When I interviewed teachers for this book, they had many stories of modeling, but they had far fewer examples of scaffolding. Yet, the combination of modeling and scaffolding is powerful. It "reduces the extraneous load on students' working memories and strengthens schema, making learning more efficient, more manageable, and easier for them to retrieve," according to Adam Riches, the author of *Teach Smarter*. These important outcomes should make us want to learn more in order to implement it well.

In their book *How Learning Happens*, Paul Kirschner and Carl Hendrick acknowledge the challenging nature of scaffolding because experiments involving helping children build a pyramid from building blocks shows that effective scaffolding is specific to the child and only provided at the point where assistance is needed. They say,

> Scaffolding is a highly complex process requiring a wide range of skills from the instructor or teacher. To properly scaffold, the teacher needs to possess and show a range of emotional skills such as empathy and patience. (S)he also needs to know when and how to provide close support and also when and how to take it away. Finally, they need to be able to hold two mental models at once; their own mental model of the overall problem to be solved and crucially, the child's mental model.

This involves a high level of individual differentiation as it involves giving the right support to the right student for the right content at exactly the right time. Such a high level of scaffolding would be difficult to accomplish in a classroom full of students. Kirschner's advice for the classroom is to teach a short lesson and then demonstrate a skill while verbalizing your thought processes followed by a good amount of time for the student to practice both with and without your assistance.

Some teachers do provide scaffolds to only some individuals and only at the point of their need. The teacher may notice, for example, that a particular student is struggling with solving a math problem that others are not having the same difficulty with and hand them a sheet with prompts to use during that day's lesson. I think this is a good practice if you have the right classroom climate, but in a world obsessed with fairness, you may want to establish expectations and explanations for this sort of thing early in the year. Another option would be to save those sorts of supports for small group instruction or individual help times when the rest of the class can't observe what you are providing. We often think of scaffolding downward to support struggling students, but you can also scaffold up to help students who finish quickly and want a challenge. Barbara Oakley and her colleagues provide some good advice for scaffolding upward in *Uncommon Sense Teaching*. Often, teachers just give them more of the same type of problem to do. These students will find that dull, even punishing. Oakley suggests asking them to generate problems, giving them a creative challenge and a way to extend their learning rather than simply repeating it.

It may appear that scaffolding is not possible during direct instruction because it would seem you need to divide students into differentiated groups. In reality, direct instruction is when the teacher is most able to manage the timing and allocation of support resources. In the article I referenced in Chapter 6, Kirschner advocates a method of scaffolding used as part of direct instruction, starting with fully worked examples and then moving to only partially worked examples. This helps move students toward independence under the teacher's careful guidance.

The method of "I do, we do, you do" comes to mind as the support moves from the teacher to the student in carefully administered doses. In *Clarity for Learning*, John Almarode and Kara Vandas describe this type of modeling and scaffolding structure as a "gradual release of responsibility," leading to more independence in the learner over time as students first observe the thinking processes necessary for success and then practice them with prompts before eventually taking on the tasks on their own. Training in many jobs involves this sort of process. If your job involves a unique computer system, the company may first provide a manual or class with instructions about their system. They may then have the new employee shadow an experienced person as they show and explain various tasks, then watch the trainee do it themselves while they provide feedback. Finally, the newly hired person takes over the post for themselves. Teachers can do the same through modeling a process to a class, then having the class perform it along with the teacher, during which he asks questions or provides prompts. Then he can have the students perform the task with a partner while circulating to provide feedback and finally doing it on their own for homework or an entrance ticket. In *Uncommon Sense Teaching*, Barbara Oakley and her colleagues describe how this gradual release process lays down and solidifies neural networks as the learning brain has to reach a little harder with each removal of support, thereby strengthening and myelinating those neurons. She recommends giving the independent practice as homework so that there is time for the brain to take advantage of diffuse mode and allow the practice to "interrupt forgetting" several hours after the initial presentation of material. Many of the skills in science classes lend themselves well to this type of process, so let's look at how some science teachers employ it.

Every science teacher I know models frequently. Anytime we introduce a new skill, we model how to do it. When the biology teacher Zane Smitley begins having his students dissect, he doesn't just hand them scalpels and set them off to hack up a specimen. He guides students through the dissection process by first showing them how to make the incisions and peel back layers of tissues for examination. When the chemistry teacher Melanie Dunning teaches stoichiometry, she models the process of moving from grams to moles of the known reagent to moles to grams of the unknown, explaining the logic of the process as she does. When I present vector resolution problems to my physics students, I model the method of using sine and cosine to break down vectors into their components.

After having modeled a process, we frequently fall into the trap of thinking that since we have modeled it, they will do it exactly the way we did and set them off to practice on their own. At least, that's the trap I fall into. It turns out not to work so well when I do it that way. Some students may have been distracted and missed a small but important step in the model. They may have misunderstood why a negative sign matters. Students have habits and preferences of their own and will usually default to them, which is fine if I only care about the answer and not the process. But for most scientific and mathematical skills, the method matters almost as much as reaching the correct conclusion, so we must support them through the entire process as they learn.

It is important to remember that students cannot see into our heads while we are showing these examples, and often, we only show them the end result of our thinking rather than the full process. They need to see the entire exercise. Therefore, explaining our thinking out loud while we are working the problem is an important part of modeling and should be done more than once. Starting with the typical and slowly introducing nuances and exceptions requires us to point out similarities and differences.

I have even found it to be valuable for students to see our recovery from mistakes during modeling. This happened a few years ago in my physics class. I was showing how to find the current and voltage in each resistor of a combination circuit, and I accidentally skipped a step in the parallel portion but didn't realize I had done it until several steps later when something didn't add up (literally). I told my students something was not right, but I would need a moment to figure out what it was. I then started at the beginning of the problem, explaining each step out loud until I got to the part where I had gone astray. When I found it, I said, "Oh, here, I see what I did wrong. Be careful about this because it is easy to miss. Let's start from here, so you can see how it affected the steps that came after it." I'm not suggesting we make mistakes on purpose just so we can model the recovery, but when we make them, we should continue to talk out loud so that students can observe how we use our mental resources to diagnose and address the mistake.

I asked every teacher I interviewed how many modeled examples they did before asking students to do it on their own. Some of them had exact numbers, but most just said, "Hmm, a lot." Nearly every teacher I spoke with used a method in which they gradually released the process from themselves to the students. The teacher shows the first example on the board while students either watch or follow along, copying the example into their notes. If it is a particularly complex skill, they may do two. For the next example, they ask students to participate in the process, asking questions like, "What do we do first?" and "What comes next?" and "What am I missing here?" Most of the teachers I talked to said they would do at least two or three of those before expecting students to practice independently. In my classes, I want that first independent practice problem to be done while they are still in the room with me, so I walk around the room with a bell and tell them to let me know when they are ready to "be dinged." It gives me a chance to look over their shoulders and see if they are making critical errors before they get too far. Even their homework is not truly independent as they have notes, worked examples in the textbook, and video resources to help them.

It is crucial that you choose your first model example well, so take time crafting it. Whatever you show students first is how they assume all the problems will work, even if that is not the case. The first example should be the stereotypical type of problem. In fact, I would say that the first few examples should be the same type of problem. As adults, we worry that this seems boring, but it doesn't feel that way to the novice learner. They need to see the pattern repeated before we start introducing nuances. When I do start introducing more complex examples to them, I say something like, "Okay, I think you have this down. Now, you are ready for me to throw a monkey wrench into the works," before showing a problem in which acceleration due to gravity is not equal to $9.8 m/s^2$ because the problem takes place on the moon. The biology teacher Zane Smitley said it well, "Start with the easiest ones before adding complexity."

If the method I am using and asking students to use is important, then I provide them with a scaffold in the early days of learning and practice. I point them to a properly worked example in the textbook or provide a video in which I modeled the process. I might write the steps at the top of the practice sheet. I want to get them to independence soon, but if I try to do it too quickly, they will give up in frustration. Scaffolds prevent giving up, and I know that better now than I did in my first years.

The earth science teacher Alyssa Powell uses diagrams, maps, and charts as scaffolds, but she includes a formative assessment where they know they will not be allowed to use them. That way, they can be prepared to do it with the knowledge in their heads before the stakes are at test-level. The biology teacher Zane Smitley uses a detailed annotated lab report model and encourages students to use it as they craft their own reports. They turn in a rough draft for his feedback before committing to the final product.

On the podcast *Tips for Teachers*, Craig Barton and Tom Sherrington discussed having a set of stock phrases or sentence stems where students can fill in the blank. For example, "I think the answer is ____, because ____." When I read their examples, one sprung to mind as especially useful. "An advantage is ____. A disadvantage is ____." This will allow them to focus on the content rather than the structure of the answer.

As I listened, I thought about the chapter I teach on electricity where we talk about alternating and direct current. There is a reason we use batteries (DC) for small and portable devices while using AC for things requiring more energy and where mobility is not an issue. It would be great during a retrieval activity to give students this kind of fill-in-the-blank stem because they wouldn't have to worry about coming up with the wording themselves. This could also work with series and parallel circuits, sources of alternative energy, and different types of joints in the body. Providing the sentence structure as a scaffold allows the student to think deeply about the content rather than how to make the answer "sound good."

Sometimes scaffolding may be about the timing of your delivery. Consider a situation where there is an exception to the rule you are teaching. First, decide whether your students need to know that or if you just find it interesting. If they are young or you are never going to assess them on the exception, they may not need to have those nuances in their working memory. If you do want them to work with the exceptions, wait until they have the rule firmly implanted before introducing the deviations from it. If you have time, consider putting them in a separate lesson on a different day.

One idea I have become interested in recently is using non-examples as part of the modeling and scaffolding process. Schema includes not only what something is but also what it isn't. A balloon animal in the shape of a giraffe is not a giraffe, but it has some similarities. Non-examples help students build their schema as they find the boundaries of a definition. This is especially useful when there are similar concepts that can be easily confused, like primary and secondary pollutants in an environmental science class or the difference between reptiles and amphibians in a middle school life science class or different types of joints in an anatomy class. Andy Tharby says non-examples will "prevent students from over-generalizing and encourage them to discriminate between similar concepts."

Again, choose your timing carefully when introducing non-examples. If you do it too early, you risk encoding the non-example rather than the actual concept. It might be useful to wait until students have slept on a concept and make the non-examples part of the next day's review time. They first need to be clear about, according to Tharby, "why right is right." At minimum, wait until you have introduced at least three or four examples of a series circuit before showing a circuit that isn't connected to a voltage source or has a parallel branch. Then, hang a bright light on the misconception and explain why it is wrong. You don't want students thinking this is another example of the right way to do it when your purpose is to show them the opposite. It would help to ask students to explain to you why it is wrong as well, or better yet, have them create examples and non-examples on their mini-whiteboards.

In *Uncommon Sense Teaching*, there is a different approach offered, however, known as conceptual attainment. It turns what I just said around, starting with the examples and non-examples before the concept has been taught. In this strategy, the examples and non-examples are presented simultaneously and sorted into groups at the beginning of the lesson. Students are then asked to generate the definition or concept themselves based on those groups. After the concept has been discussed, the teacher gives more examples and non-examples as a test of their understanding. In Craig Barton's book *Tips for Teachers*, he describes how to use this in math lessons. He provides one example at a time and asks them to give a thumbs up or down as to whether the example fits the category. If there is a disparity of answers, they discuss. Then he tells them the correct answer before moving on to the next example or non-example. As they build their list, patterns emerge, and the concept can be attained. The example I used from Hannah Eichhorst's classroom in Chapter 3 represents a sort of blend of these two methods. Because she had first presented the concept of cells and living things, she isn't quite having them start from nothing but examples to generate an understanding. When she had students generate the list and included their unintentional non-examples into a second list, they were able to solidify their attainment of the concept as they figured out that living things have cells and nonliving things do not.

In the chapter on clarity, I mentioned how Zane ensures his students can gauge their accuracy with lab report graphs by using a carefully crafted model, but I didn't mention that he employs non-examples to help with this as well. After he has taught them all of the elements that should be included in a proper graph—title, scale, units, and so on—and they have practiced making graphs correctly several times, he shows them a graph with an element or two missing and asks them to identify what is wrong with it. Non-examples like these will only work where there are clear defining lines and where small differences could be easily confused by students, leading them to wrong conclusions. Use them thoughtfully rather than throwing them into every lesson.

Scaffolding is not simply one thing. Whether it is a diagram or chart that students have temporary access or a graphic organizer that helps compare and contrast content for study purposes or breaking down a process into parts before asking students to put the entire process together on their own, any support you give to students during the initial stages of their learning that is removed after they become more proficient is a scaffold. It is not necessary to provide one for every student for every new skill, but it is worth thinking about when they might be useful and incorporating them into your lesson plans ahead of time rather than waiting until students struggle.

Coming up with multiple models and scaffolds, especially if you are expected to differentiate for a variety of learning levels, can be time-consuming. There are multiple resources available with a range of quality levels, so use your professional judgment in finding them, editing them, and using them with your students. One of the best resources to consider is the teacher in your school whose specialty is working with the students who have special needs. They have great ideas for helping students organize content and often help them to create scaffolds for themselves if the teacher has not provided them. Go to them and find a source of practical wisdom.

8 When to Memorize

During the chapter on chemical bonding, my eighth-grade students are required to memorize twelve polyatomic ions, and they do not find it easy. I understand why they find ammonium (NH_4^{+1}) and acetate ($C_2H_3O_2^{-1}$) difficult, but some of them are fairly simple and paired, like sulfate and sulfite, phosphate and phosphite, and nitrate and nitrite. Nonetheless, they balk at it every year. Two years ago, we experienced a large number of schedule interruptions during the time of the bonding chapter. From parent–teacher conferences (which were expected) to a late night storm knocking out the power in the school building (which was not expected), it felt like that chapter was not meant to have any degree of flow. As a result, I could never plan a day to have the polyatomic ion quiz. As a result, I did something I had never done before. For the first time in twenty-three years of teaching, I told them they didn't have to have the ions memorized and that I would provide a reference list on their test in the same way I give physics students an equations list. I thought it would be fine since they had the list to refer to, but I was wrong. My students performed quite poorly that year on every one of the questions that included polyatomic ions, far worse than the years in which they had been required to memorize them. I was flabbergasted and said to them, "I don't understand. You had the list in your hands." One of the most insightful students said, "I never looked at it because I didn't know when I needed to look at it." Because they had not memorized them, they didn't recognize them.

If you have been in education for more than a couple of years, you have likely been told that information acquisition isn't necessary in a world where the internet exists. You may have even been enticed by the idea because it is appealing to think I can have my students focus only on the higher levels of Bloom's taxonomy. But if you tried it, you know it resulted in high degrees of student frustration and did not result in much learning. Asking your students to compare and contrast things they have just looked up provides a shallow result. Asking them to synthesize it is unfair to them because they don't have enough knowledge in their minds to integrate. Evaluation and creation seem to be impossible with things you do not have stored in your brain.

As Carl Hendrick put it, "The most important memory is still the one inside your head." Having things in long-term memory matters. No matter what our access is to information, some things just have to be in our brains to be useful. The illustration I use with my students is the act of reading without having a vocabulary. Since the first publication of the dictionary, we have been able to look up unfamiliar words, but imagine how difficult and meaningless reading would be if you had to do that more than a few times while reading an article. Even if you only had to pause to Google the definition of a word once per page, it would seriously hamper your understanding and enjoyment of the piece you were reading. In Chapter 2 of *Why Don't Students Like School*, Daniel Willingham puts it well, saying "There is no doubt that having students memorize lists of isolated facts is not enriching. It is also true (though less often appreciated) that trying to teach students skills such as analysis or synthesis in the absence of factual knowledge is impossible."

The foundation that allows progress to become visible is often invisible itself. I pass a construction site daily on my way to the YMCA. First they tore down the previous building and dug a very deep hole. For a few weeks after that, it seemed like no progress was being made on the construction of an actual structure. A few days ago, I noticed how quickly the building is progressing as it now rises twelve stories above me. Did they take a long break after digging the hole? No, they laid rebar and poured concrete into the hole and gave it time to cure in order to set the foundation. Progress was being made, but it wasn't visible because it was happening below the surface. The concrete that was poured deep into the ground provided the support needed for everything that has come after. Once it was set, the building progressed quickly. This put me in mind of a 2019 conference session with Barbara Oakley. In it, she said, "There are people who will tell you students should not have to learn anything they can Google. Don't fall for that." She talked about the neurological changes that happen in our brains when we memorize and how that process is necessary for higher-level thinking. She went on to compare the non-memorizing approach to building a house without a foundation. It may look good for a while, but without the support of the foundation, the house quickly crumbles. If the construction workers on the site I pass had wanted the appearance of quick progress, they certainly could have had it by starting the above ground work as soon as the debris from the old structure was hauled away. But it wouldn't have looked good for long because the building would not have maintained its structural integrity. Learning without a knowledge foundation may look good, but it doesn't last.

Having students working together on projects certainly looks good when a tour is coming through the building or when you are being observed by an administrator, but can those people tell if your students are learning anything that lasts? If students are asked questions about their learning, will it still look good or will it crumble without the foundation needed for understanding. Memorization isn't something schools post on their social media pages or use in fundraising literature because it doesn't look progressive and can't be captured in photographs, but it is a time-tested method of learning that has served us well for thousands of years.

The disdain for memorization is a fairly recent development. People used to prize their ability to memorize large amounts of information and recall them at will. That ability then allowed them to use what they knew in novel situations and allude to them in creative works of art, poetry, and song. And, of course, there are still competitions around the world in which memory champions learn long lists of words, decks of playing cards, the names of roomfuls of people, trivia, and even abstract images. In *International Journal of Applied Research*, Dr. Md. Enamul Hoque says,

> Informed educators are often quick to write off rote memorization as an unnecessary and even harmful exercise, instead preferring to teach creativity and problem solving. While we agree that creative, analytical lessons are a great way to learn, it's worth pointing out that memorization can still play an important role in learning, no matter your age. Memorization should not be ignored at all.

He compares memorization—a mental exercise—to body movement—a physical exercise, training the brain to be more susceptible to remembering future information. He also reminds us that memorization doesn't have to rely on rote methods alone and encourages readers to find the most efficient and effective way possible to use memorization in order to experience the benefits of having knowledge inside one's own mind. He suggests that memorization benefits us by challenging our brains, improving neuroplasticity, teaching patterns, freeing up space in the working memory, practicing focus, learning more complex conceptual information, and increasing the agility of the brain.

In his article "Powerful Knowledge, Educational Potential and Knowledge-Rich Curriculum: Pushing the Boundaries," Zongyi Deng says, "In classrooms, the primary task of a teacher is to help students to acquire a body of disciplinary knowledge and to take them beyond their everyday experience" and makes the point that it gives us a shared vocabulary for engaging in discussion. In a study of over two thousand students, a knowledge-rich curriculum beginning in kindergarten was shown to improve reading comprehension with the effect being especially dramatic for students of lower opportunity backgrounds. This tells me that abandoning memorization may only serve to increase education gaps, causing further disadvantages to those for whom education should be most helpful.

I've been trying not to give too many wonky details in this book about neuroscience because my aim is to focus on practical advice, but you just have to be patient with me on this one because I think it is fascinating. You may remember from the introduction that it was a book on neuroplasticity that started me on the road to studying how we learn in the first place, so give me a second to amaze you with what happens to our neurons when we learn, albeit massively oversimplified.

When a student learns something new, dendrites change shape and length, reorganizing communication within the brain. According to a March 2010 article in *Trends in Neurosciences*, "Recent studies show that dendritic spines are dynamic structures. Their rapid creation, destruction and shape-changing are essential for short- and long-term plasticity at excitatory synapses on pyramidal neurons in the cerebral cortex" and "spine dynamics are cellular phenomena with important implications for cognition and memory." I think it is phenomenal that scientists have found physical manifestations of learning, even if I don't yet know how to take advantage of that finding. The more dendrites there are and the more interconnected they become with each other, the more efficient learning becomes. I would suggest that it also enables more creative thought as previously unconnected parts of the brain are now able to communicate. In his book *How We Learn*, Stanislas Dehaene states, "Single neurons may provide some information, but an overall memory is always encoded by several interconnected groups of neurons." This is the physical aspect of the schema building process we talked about in Chapter 3. Perhaps, something I learned today about math will connect with something I learned last year about art or history or language, causing schemas to overlap and allowing me to have an insight I didn't previously have, all thanks to learning new information and its effect on my growing, ever-changing dendrites.

When practicing a new skill or rehearsing information, the myelin layer around the neuron thickens (myelination), enabling faster communication the next time that pathway is activated. In physical skills, we call it muscle memory, but muscles don't remember things as they are just meat. This thing we call muscle memory is simply a well-myelinated pathway, made of multiple neurons. According to Stanislas Dehaene, the physical changes in a neuron when memorizing and practicing, strengthen the interconnections between them, "making it more likely that this set of neurons will fire in the future."

Indulge me in another kickboxing example. In Matt's class, the routine is changed every six weeks or so. When we first start a new routine, we are an absolute mess. Hardly anyone in the class is doing the same thing as our Matt, in spite of the fact that he is cueing it well. Two weeks later, most of us are getting it mostly right most of the time because we now have pathways that connect one move to the next due to myelination. Just as this works in physical activity, it also works in academic learning. As we retrieve the memory, we grow the myelin, allowing us to retrieve it more efficiently the next time we need it. According to R. Douglas Fields's article in *Nature Reviews Neuroscience*, myelination is activity dependent. Thus, the old adage "if you don't use it, you lose it" is true because when we don't practice something, we lose myelin or don't myelinate the neuron in the first place.

There is one more interesting thing that is happening when we memorize, and this is the study that affirmed my intuition that students couldn't engage in higher-level thinking without memorizing things first. According to a Princeton University model of neural networks in learning, the hippocampus (where working memory is sorted) is easily overwhelmed by new learning and must send it to the neocortex for storage (long-term memory). But the brain has to know where to store the new learning, so it takes advantage of two synaptic pathways in the brain to compare and contrast the new learning with previously known information. In Kevin Washburn's book *The Architecture of Learning*, he describes how memorizing new material helps with schema building by expressing the brain's role as a pattern recognition device. He says, "The brain receives and sorts sensory data, causing patterns to emerge. The patterns direct the brain to search its long-term memory stores for previous experiences that illustrate similar patterns." That means that the act of memorizing already involves the higher-level thinking skills of comparing and contrasting just to know how to store it. Memory is aided by the recognition of patterns, and it only recognizes them after it has been memorized and made part of the existing schema.

Memorization Techniques

(Definitely NOT a complete list - add your own!)

Mnemonic Devices
Chunking
Telling Someone Else
Mental Imagery
Repetition
Summarizing to Focus on Meaning
Connection to Emotion
Memory Palace
Jingles and Chants
Metaphors
Rote Repetition

Figure 8.1 Memorization techniques.

As I mentioned earlier, rote memorization is not the only way of storing information in our minds. This is where memorization advocates and detractors can find common ground. We know that information is better remembered when connected to meaning. As Washburn says, "Data not processed is short-lived." He makes the point that knowledge and thinking cannot be separated from each other if there is meaning to the content, which is why we often talk to ourselves while attempting to learn something new. Rote memory is only best used when the content has no meaning that would lead to remembering it better. For example, I want my students to know that radio waves are the longest in the electromagnetic spectrum and gamma rays are the shortest. This matters because radio waves are great for the study of distant stars because of their long wavelength, and gamma rays carry higher health risk to our cells because of their short wavelength. There is not, however, any meaning that connects wavelength to the name of the wave. In that case, rote memory is really our best option, perhaps even using a mnemonic device. For content that has depth of meaning, it is rather useful to have students connect their memorizing to that meaning.

Flashcards often seem like they only allow for rote memory, but in his book *Outsmart Your Brain*, Daniel Willingham proposes a way to make them more useful. He says, "There's no reason you can't pose and answer conceptual questions in a flashcard format, including essay questions. This is getting you thinking about themes and connecting big ideas, and that's going to be useful for studying." After reading Willingham's book, I encouraged my students to slow down in their flashcard study sessions. I advised them to pause between cards and ask, "What makes that true? Why is that the answer? Why isn't it a different answer?" By pausing to think about the meaning of the answer, students will be more likely to remember the answer itself. In *How We Learn*, Stanislas Dehaene describes how brain imaging reveals this "processing depth effect," explaining that deeper processing activities activate areas of the prefrontal cortex that form loops with the hippocampus. He does not advise one preferred method of deep processing but says that "all solutions that force students to give up the comfort of passivity are effective."

So, we agree that you need to have your students memorize some things, but they don't need instant recall of everything. How do you decide? When I interviewed Hannah Eichhorst, I asked what she had students memorize, and her answer was "as little as possible." When she described her retrieval activities during class, however, I realized they are memorizing things without her calling it that and without her assigning them things to memorize that she will later quiz them on. It looks different in her classroom than mine, but they are encoding things into long-term memory nonetheless. Other teachers I spoke to were at the opposite end of the spectrum, having students memorize a lot in order to free up working memory. Part of the difference in these answers is due to the age level of their students and the complexity of their material, and part of it is just the personality of each teacher. Not one teacher that I interviewed said that they don't have students memorize anything because they can "just look it up."

So how does a teacher decide? What needs to be firmly in memory? What is it okay to look up? When should I provide a reference sheet of equations and constants? When should I expect them to know those things without help?

I was once listening to a presentation by Kevin Washburn at a convention of the Association of Christian School International (ACSI) and found his take extremely helpful. He said,

> When educators talk about memorizing, it's usually with a scowl. "Memorizing is so beneath us. We don't have students memorize anything. Everything we teach is meaningful. It's all the others—teachers who teach other disciplines—who make students memorize unnecessary information. We're above such an approach." But let's be honest. Despite the fact that most everything factual can now be found quickly via technology, some information still possesses its greatest value when it

is memorized. At its best, memorizing enables efficiency in thinking and acting.

The phrase "memorizing enables efficiency in thinking" stuck with me, so I sent him a message on Facebook to ask him about it. In his reply, he said I should ask the question, "What do I want them to do with what they have memorized?" If I want them to plug something into an equation, like the gravitational constant in a calculation of the force between masses, it is probably not necessary to have them memorize it. It's more important that they recognize the relationship between masses and the distance between them. If, however, I want them to compare DNA with RNA and how they function in our genetics, they need to have a firm knowledge of each of those things separately. Otherwise, there will be no fluidity of thought in their comparison.

There are chemistry teachers who have their students memorize the entire periodic table, including the atomic numbers, masses, symbols, and placements of each element. If you are one of those teachers, I apologize for thinking that you are a little nutty. It's a tool to be used, and Mendeleev himself would tell you so. I would never dream of making them memorize the numbers because its purpose is to be a reference tool for those numbers. I do, however, have students memorize the symbols of the sixty most commonly used elements. I do this because it "enables efficiency." When I ask the question about what I want them to do with these memorized symbols, the answer is that I want them to be able to use the periodic table efficiently. It allows students to use the tool more fluently if they aren't wasting time looking for sodium by searching for the letters So when its symbol is Na. We make flashcards and drill them (rote), pausing to talk about the Latin roots of some of the symbols (reflecting on meaning), and have a quiz (retrieval). But I make sure I communicate to them that the reason I have them memorize them is to make using the tool more efficient, not because I think it is fun to know that the symbol for gold is Au.

In my physics class, I make the choice not to have my students memorize equations, but I understand why some physics teachers do. I think you can make the argument either way on this one, but I have decided that teaching them to decide which equation to use is more important than having them recall the equation. If you are a teacher who has them memorize the equations, you aren't wrong to do so. Perhaps, your students have a better understanding of the physical relationships than mine do. As long as we have each examined our goals and can back up our policies with reasoning, I think we can both benefit our students. The AP biology teacher, Zane Smitley, told me that he does not have them memorize information that will be provided by College Board on the AP exam. This is reasonable as they get practice in using the resource that will be available to them during the assessment. He does, however, make students memorize processes and the vocabulary associated with those processes. In his words, "If they don't memorize the vocabulary, they'll be lost when I'm talking because I will use those words a lot."

Zane also teaches anatomy, and those students memorize large amounts of information, from Latin roots and prefixes to the names of bones and muscles to types of tissues. Why do they need to memorize them rather than refer to a chart posted in the room? Because he is going to use words like ulna, adductor, epithelial, and foramen frequently. If students don't have the definitions of those words firmly in their long-term memory and have to reference a diagram or look it up in a glossary, it will slow their ability to process lessons. He would have to pause mid-sentence to allow them to look it up or put them at risk of missing what he says in the rest of the sentence. I watch them go through diagrams, vocabulary lists, and flashcards as they study for his quizzes, but I also see them come in after school to handle bones, seeing the connections at the proximal and distal ends, recognizing how their body functions in a different way. I've seen them create artwork of accurately drawn hearts and sculptures of imaginary creatures using the joints they have learned. Having this information memorized enables creativity and understanding in a way looking it up in the book or a website would not. He then has them use their understanding in dissection and projects, including one where students must create a "murder scene" and plant evidence that requires other students to use their knowledge to solve the crime. Having the knowledge in their heads allows them to know what questions to ask about the evidence.

As I write this, I am sitting in Zane's classroom, listening to him interact with Addie, an AP biology student with a high level of motivation. She has come in on her own time because she is preparing for the AP biology exam. Right now, they are discussing cellular respiration. He is asking profound questions about the process while she draws information from her memory and connects it together to synthesize it into a deep understanding. She just said, "I thought this happened because ..." and he confirmed that this was the conclusion he was hoping she would draw. As she stands here, talking about oxidation, ATP, energy storage, and the movement of molecules and electrons in the respiration process and using that to draw high-level conclusions, I am struck by the thought that there is no way she could be engaging at this level if she were constantly having to look up each term or Google each process. Because this information is already in her long-term memory, it is available for higher-level thinking. It reminded me of a quote from Ulrich Kraft, in his *Scientific American* article "Unleashing Creativity." In it, he analyzes our current understanding of where creativity comes from. The statement, "Fresh solutions result from disassembling and reassembling the building blocks in an infinite number of ways. That means the problem solver must thoroughly understand the blocks." So, before you race quickly up the Bloom's pyramid, rushing your students toward synthesis, evaluation, and creativity, it is important to remember that those thinking levels require efficiency of thought that only comes from having knowledge in long-term memory. So, the answer to the question "what do they need to memorize" has a simple answer. Have them memorize whatever information you want them to think with at a later date.

Those polyatomic ions I mentioned at the beginning of the chapter will show up for three more chapters in physical science and for the rest of the year in chemistry, and it will slow them down if they constantly need to look them up. And, as I mentioned earlier, they may not even know when to look them up because they may not recognize the difference between a polyatomic ion and separate elements. Their performance was worse when I put the list in their hands because they didn't recognize them. I find value in students having those in their heads because of the number of times I know they will need them and because of their need to recognize them on sight. If they were only going to apply to a few examples in one chapter, I would probably make a different choice. You can make a different choice in your classroom. Perhaps you want them to have the layers of the atmosphere down cold so that you can ask them higher-level questions that would be difficult to answer if they were slowed down by looking up the features of each layer. Perhaps you have a student who would benefit from a simplified reference chart of the layers. It's up to you, but don't be afraid to have them memorize just because it has recently gone out of fashion.

This is an area where your professional judgment is crucial. Trust your training, the advice of experienced teachers, and your own experience. Don't make decisions based on what the current fad says you should do because it will be gone soon while the lessons from your experience remain. Don't be afraid to change your mind next year if you decide it would have been better to have made a different decision. Experience should change your judgment because you will often recognize the impact of the decision you made and wish it had come out differently. Back up what you decide with reasons, and most people will respect your thought process even if they disagree with your conclusion.

9 Retrieval Practice

Let me take you back to my cardio kickboxing class one more time. It is an energetic class with fun music and dance-y punches and kicks, where I grin from ear to ear and never once look up at the clock. This is largely due to Matt, who is one of the most naturally gifted educators I've ever met. In spite of his having no training in teaching methods, I watch him use sound practices every week. In each kickboxing class, after having done a combination move a few times, Matt stops and watches us do it without his cues, joking that we won't need him anymore. I hate it when he does that because I'm pretty sure I'm going to be the one who skips a step or uppercuts in the wrong direction, but I respect him for doing it because it improves our performance for the next week. He giggles at the look of panic on our faces as soon as he stops talking, but he instinctively knows this method helps us. He has likely not read books about retrieval practice, but he is employing it well. Recent research has shown that it is one of our most powerful educational tools.

According to the website RetrievalPractice.org, "Retrieval practice is a strategy of deliberately bringing information to mind," and it is a powerful tool for memory and fluency. Even if you didn't know the term before, you would know what it is. You did it in school; we all did. You have probably heard it downplayed as "drill and kill." (Why do we think anything that rhymes is true? Can we have equal impact if we use a rhyme, like "drill for skill"?) You have likely been advised not to use it because "it is boring." You also know it works. While we typically think of flashcards and whiteboards for retrieval, there are many other methods, and using a variety can engage students in retrieval practice while preventing boredom. I've certainly never been bored in Matt's class when he engages us in retrieval. On the contrary, I feel empowered to succeed on my own.

Researcher Pooja Agarwal did something most other researchers have not. She partnered with Patrice Bain, a teacher in an actual classroom, to study retrieval practice "in the wild." Prior to this partnership, all the research done on retrieval was done with college students in laboratory settings using lists of words rather than academic content. Those experiments probably yielded some results, but they did not help teachers know how to apply their findings in their own classrooms, where the conditions are far from controlled and content is not held in a tidy list. Lab experiments did not include nuances that a teacher would encounter, like content of varying complexity or how things might change if you only had five minutes to engage in retrieval activities in one class while you had eleven minutes in another. The Agarwal and Bain partnership gives more practical results because the research was carried out for several years with Patrice Bain's real students and her real content.

They found that the energy it takes to try to remember something is useful for remembering it again in the future. In their book *Powerful Teaching*, Agarwal and Bain go as far as to say we should focus on the retrieval stage, not the encoding stage. That is not to say that the encoding stage is unimportant, but encoding becomes lost if we don't put effort into practicing the retrieval of that which we have encoded. They say, "Retrieval practice boosts learning by pulling information out of students' heads, rather than cramming information into students' heads. Just like students practice an instrument, they need to practice their knowledge, too." They advise that teachers view encoding and retrieval as partners that go hand in hand and to look for ways to intersperse retrieval during the encoding process because "when students are retrieving, they are also encoding."

The typical progression has been putting stuff in and waiting until later to ask students to retrieve it. Agarwal and Bain found that this is not the most effective practice; there must be an interaction between what we are learning and what we already know, so they advise sprinkling retrieval throughout the learning process.

Experiments were set up in Patrice Bain's classes during which students were quizzed over what they were learning throughout a part of the lesson while the other part of the lesson was presented in a normal direct instruction manner. When the students were tested at the end of the unit, they remembered 81 percent of the information that had been presented without quizzing, but they remembered 94 percent of the material on which they had been quizzed. The difference between the two sections was even more dramatic when they took another test at the end of the semester. Those who engaged in retrieval during their instruction forgot less than the control group. Their conclusion from this experiment and others was that retrieval practice had powerful effects for both short-term assessments and long-term learning.

This impact has been replicated by others across multiple academic levels. In a study of college students taking statistics for psychology, one section of the course served as the experimental group who were required to answer a set of questions that caused them to retrieve content from that day's lesson while the control group section ended class as they usually would. The exam scores were significantly higher in the section engaged in retrieval practice. Medical school students who used apps like Anki, which prompts multiple choice retrieval at spaced intervals, achieved higher scores on medical licensing exams than those who studied without such apps. Anecdotally, when I mentioned Anki once on social media, I got a flood of comments from both medical and law students, telling me it was their primary tool for studying high volumes of memorized information because they could retrieve on their phones while standing in line at the grocery store or while riding a train to work. It is nice to know that research has spanned many levels with varying types of content and with all types of questioning methods. As a teacher, that leaves me confident I can apply it to my setting and curriculum as well.

While the most straightforward way to engage in retrieval is the good old fashioned flashcard, it is not the only way to engage in retrieval. Remember, retrieval is any way that we get students to find the information in their brain rather than an external source. Non-flashcard methods may be helpful in going deeper than the remembering level. In an experiment carried out in Spain, psychology researchers Lechuga, Ortega-Tudela, and Gómez-Ariza used retrieval based concept mapping to help students retrieve and find themes in their learning. Participants in the experiment were asked to read a text and then retrieve information from them. For one text, students first engaged in what I would call a brain bomb, freely recalling all the information they could by writing down as many things as they could remember without regard to theme or flow. Later, they were asked to retrieve it in the form of a concept map. For the second text, they engaged in the same activities, but the order was reversed. Those who engaged in the concept map before free recall performed significantly better on a test of their learning two weeks later than those who did it in the reverse order. They did not speculate in their paper about why the order mattered, but as I read the study, I thought about Daniel Willingham's famous phrase, "Memory is the residue of thought." He suggests that students will always remember more if they have taken the time to think about the meaning of the content while memorizing it. Perhaps the implication of the Spanish study is that those who engaged in the concept mapping first had primed their brains to focus on meaning each time they retrieved in the future while those who waited to think about meaning lost that benefit during the free retrieval activity.

Retrieval can serve to give a more accurate picture of our learning, not just to the teacher but to the student as well. As humans, we are not generally great at assessing our own learning. We tend to overestimate how well we know something before we are asked to retrieve it or use it to solve problems. Students often enter a test situation very confident, only to be disappointed by their score. They misled themselves because they had recognition of topics rather than actual knowledge of specifics. You may have noticed this if you have ever used the "thumbs up, thumbs down" form of self-assessment, which I'll address again in Chapter 10. The experiments carried out with retrieval practice show that studying with retrieval allows them to more accurately evaluate what they know and what they do not know because they have tried to remember and then received feedback on their accuracy. Leaving space between the retrieval sessions further increases their ability to be sure of what they know because if they remember it two minutes after seeing it, they may just not have yet dropped it from their working memory. If they still remember it a day later or a week later, they have committed it to their long-term memory. Psychologist Bradley Bush once tweeted that because retrieval practice "aids learning and reduces uncertainty," it is especially powerful for students with testing anxiety. Since retrieval practice is such a winning strategy, let's talk about multiple ways to incorporate it into your daily routines.

When the "testing effect" of retrieval practice was first introduced in the literature, we, as teachers, went way too far with it. Part of the reason was the terrible name chosen by publishers. Teachers thought they needed to test their students all of the time, and we overloaded our students with pretests, retrieval tests, and summative tests. In the process, we increased stress and decreased performance. In a culture that is already a little testing crazy, we added to the crazy. But it doesn't have to look like that. Maybe, we should stop calling it the testing effect and call it something less intimidating, like a checkpoint. I rarely give pretests, not because I don't believe they are helpful, but because there are only so many minutes in the school day. When I do give them, I do not call them pretests. I call them "See What You Know Activities" and I put them on a game site like Kahoot! or Quizizz to do on their own and reduce the anxiety that would come with using the dreaded "T word."

Ever since I read *Powerful Teaching*, I have looked for ways to incorporate it wherever I can in a wide variety of ways. If you are thinking that there isn't time in your class to add this, I have two thoughts for you. First, you don't have time not to do it. Engaging in retrieval practice improves student fluency and performance on "higher-level" tasks, so it saves you time in the long run. Second, you don't have to add something new if you can modify things you are already doing to make them more effective.

I have, for example, used bellwork (or starters, catalysts, do nows, sponges—different names for the same thing in different classrooms) for my entire career because I was taught to do it in my college classroom management course using the late Harry Wong's book *The First Days of School*. In order to make room for retrieval practice, I modified the bellwork I had been using into three retrieval questions, so it takes no more class time than the bellwork was already taking. The questions depend on the lesson for the day. If it is something relatively complicated that relies on knowledge from yesterday's lesson, all three questions will be related. If not, I may take advantage of the spacing effect and pull questions from a previous week or chapter so that they keep retrieving things that I know they'll need later. I am in a one-to-one laptop school, so I use the free version of GoFormative for these questions, allowing me to set it in such a way as to give them the correct answers after they submit, allowing for instant feedback. This platform also allows me to track trends in wrong answers, so I know what I need to ask again later. It is designed to be used for formative assessment, so it is useful in multiple ways. There are also sites like Carousel, Desmos, Khan Academy, and IXL (for math questions), Socrative, and Quizlet, and so on, that can help you with the answer collection process. Getting answers from all students enables everyone to benefit.

While tech tools are helpful for tracking, they are not necessary. If your students don't have access to a device or you just don't want them to use them, you can always write the questions on the board. Alyssa Powell projects her opening questions, which she calls a "catalyst," and has the students write them on paper. Melanie Dunning provides them with a printed list at the beginning of each unit and has them answer it on that, turning them in when they have completed all of them. There are many ways to do retrieval, so feel free to be as technology-centered or paper-centered as you are comfortable with.

This leads to my favorite tool, which I have already mentioned a number of times, student mini-whiteboards. If you don't have a class set of whiteboards,

I highly recommend that you invest in them. You can buy them in bulk along with markers and eraser cloths online. I've never had such a simple tool make so much impact on the way I engage with students during a lesson. The expectation in my room is that when I ask a whiteboard question, everyone must answer. They cannot just write IDK or leave it blank. Instead of getting one answer from the student who always raises his hand or from cold calling, I am getting answers from every student. I have to shout out to Craig Barton and Adam Boxer because, while I had used whiteboards for test review before, it was their conversation on Craig's *Tips for Teachers* podcast that convinced me it was time to put a whiteboard on every desk. With whiteboards, it takes just a few seconds for my students to engage in retrieval and for me to identify and address misconceptions. It is engagement, retrieval practice, formative assessment, and feedback using a tool that's been around for ages. Are some kids copying after others raise their boards? Of course, they are. Is that still better than what they weren't doing before? Of course, it is.

Zane Smitley, the biology teacher next door to me, is the master of the mini-whiteboard. I observed him once and realized that I wasn't getting everything out of the whiteboards that I could be. He doesn't just use them to retrieve but to have them predict. Biology is so full of complex processes (photosynthesis, the Krebs cycle, respiration, cell division) that he can say, "What do you think will happen next?" and get them to process their thinking through writing or drawing. They do Punnet squares and other types of skills on them. He plans several questions ahead of time to make sure all sections are getting the questions he considers most essential, but, as a responsive educator, he also builds questions from their answers. He uses them multiple times a day, whether as part of the plan or just because he noticed their attention is waning.

I recently talked about my love of whiteboards in a faculty meeting, and Megan, our seventh-grade English teacher, decided to try it. She came to me two weeks later, gushing about what a game changer it was for her class. As we compared the kinds of questions each of us asks for whiteboard retrieval, we were able to give each other new ideas. She also said, "The best part is I am finally hearing from my introverts. They'll write down insightful things they would never say out loud." I had noticed that too. Using mini-whiteboards brings out the shy kids and creates a quiet outlet for those who are anything but shy. It gets quiet for a moment while they write, and when they hold them up, I might see something very insightful from Avrie, the quiet child who would never raise her hand to answer a question out loud.

Depending on the context, I can acknowledge her quietly with a nod or a wink or I can verbalize her awesome insight for everyone's benefit. Jonah, the student who likes to needle me by answering "beaker" for every question, can do so on his whiteboard without disrupting everyone else by saying it aloud, although I do insist that he put his real answer alongside the joke. Kolton, that student whose handwriting is illegible, gets a little gentle teasing from me when I say, "I'm sorry, but I can't read Ancient Sanskrit. What do these hieroglyphics mean?" before he says his answer out loud, at which time I can usually make out a few of the letters he meant to write. Without a struggle, he has answered more questions out loud than I would ever have gotten him to before using this method.

I could go on for a while about mini-whiteboards, but let me get back to describing retrieval techniques that don't add to your load. I try to time my classes from bell to bell, but there is always one class that finishes a little earlier than the others or took longer on one example problem so there wasn't time for another. To the annoyance of most middle and high school teachers, the students immediately want to pack up and line up at the door. I don't allow that. I take those couple of minutes as an opportunity for extra retrieval practice. If they have quick access to paper (pre-COVID-19, I velcroed baskets down to their tables with stacks of quartered looseleaf), you can say, "Write down two things you remember from today's lesson" and then take it up as an exit ticket. If you have a little more time, you can say "Brain Bomb!" and have them keep writing about anything they remember from the current chapter until the bell rings. I experimented with giving retrieval activities as homework assignments, but they just copied things, so it was not actually an act of retrieval. When they are in front of me, I can tell they aren't looking things up.

One of my favorite techniques from *Powerful Teaching* is called "Big Basket of Questions." The way I apply this technique is to print some questions, vocabulary words, examples, and other cues for myself. Then I cut them into strips and put them in a basket. At any free moment, I can pull questions from the basket and have students answer them, using their whiteboards or a digital tool or cold calling. The method I use usually depends on how much time we have because it takes time to log into a website for only a couple of questions.

It may seem that retrieval practice is all taking place at the remembering level. Even if it were, it would have value, but it doesn't have to be. As I described earlier, my biology teacher friend, who no one has ever thought of as "too easy," uses it for summarizing, predicting, and analyzing. Hannah Eichhorst gave me a great idea to use in retrieval practice as well. She shows students a diagram with wrong things and says, "There are five errors. Tell me how to fix them." Students must retrieve the right information to recognize what is wrong and correct it. When I interviewed her, I said, "I will absolutely try this next week," and I think you should consider it too. I asked her if she thought her students recognized the value of retrieval practice, and she said, "No, they hate it. That's why I disguise it in games and ways to tell me I'm wrong." By the way, I asked that question to every teacher I interviewed. Their answers correlated directly to the age of the students they taught. Elementary school and early middle school teachers said their students did not recognize it; they just thought it was difficult. Those who taught eighth grade and freshman said, "They don't love it, but they eventually see its value." Those who taught sophomores, juniors, and seniors said that their students may not love doing it but did acknowledge that it was more helpful than other practices. Zane Smitley gives his high school students an end-of-semester survey which asks, "What is one thing you think I should continue doing?" In the past two years, the most frequent answer from his high school students was "Keep the retrieval boards. They help a lot."

Another interesting way to incorporate retrieval practice into your classroom is to engage in "retrieval note taking." In this method, students do not take notes during the lesson. They pay full attention to what the teacher is doing. Then, they are given time either at the end of the lesson, at key points during the lesson, or for homework to retrieve what they remember. While I have found it difficult to work the summary into the lesson and often run out of time for it, it has the potential to be a powerful tool when done consistently. The AP physics teacher Marriana Ruggerio allowed me to pull some practices from her blog *Physics Teacher Momma*. She said this about retrieval note taking. "I've learned that the right kind of extra time always pays off in the end, and this is a perfect example." She provides a packet for her students so they can get an idea of what they will need to retrieve, helping to reduce the cognitive load they experience while she delivers the information. She also gives them time to look at each other's retrieval notes to recognize and fill in any gaps in their own and puts her slides back on the screen for the same reason. Alyssa Powell has a modified version of this as she gives her middle school students a study guide made of retrieval questions several days before they have a chapter test. They are able to retrieve what they have already learned and see the types of questions they will soon be asked on the remaining content, so it is retrieval and priming in one tool.

It takes a while for me to convince my students that they should not look up the answers for the bellwork retrieval. They are used to expectations of product rather than process and don't ever want to be wrong. I spend some time in the first days of school explaining why we do bellwork and what the purpose of trying to remember it is. Since I teach science, I have the luxury of explaining a little neuroscience to them and talking to them about myelination. When I see them looking things up during bellwork the next week, I remind them that I would rather they try to remember and get it wrong than to look things up because the first has an effect on their brain and the second is a waste of time. If they have been at my school more than two years, they were also taught the value of retrieval practice in their sixth-grade school success class. This does make the idea more credible for some because they hear it from multiple sources. The more teachers you can get using the same language, the better. Cassidy Scholten told me she faces the same issue in sixth-grade classes, where they have a warm-up journal. They want to be right, so they want to look up the answers, even though they know they will be allowed to correct their answers just a few minutes later when they go over them together in class. It takes a lot of training to convince students that it is better for their brains to try to remember. Keep retrieval opportunities as low stakes as possible. Almost all of mine are ungraded activities because they are less likely to look things up if they don't feel the pressure of a graded response. I don't know that I will ever completely overcome their compulsion to look things up, but I try to make headway.

In *Uncommon Sense Teaching*, Barbara Oakley, Beth Rogowski, and Terrence Sejnowski suggest using "think pair share" as an act of retrieval practice. You can teach a lesson, put kids into pairs, and ask them to summarize the lesson to each other. If you have time, you could ask them to write a summary together so both are contributing to the product. This would be a great technique to use after a homework assignment that involved reading a passage since many students read texts to check it off their list rather than reading for understanding. If they know they have to explain what they read to a classmate as the first activity of the next day's class, they might attend to it more carefully. The act of producing that summary will cause them to think about the meaning of what they read as they reconstruct it with their partner, and one may remember something the other didn't, helping them to see more in the text than they originally might have.

Retrieval practice is simply the best way for students to study. Flashcards aren't flashy, but they are effective, and we can teach our students to make them even more powerful. In my study skills elective, I teach seventh- and eighth-grade students about how to increase their efficiency in studying. Most of them come in with the belief that they can just "look over their notes." Since my school has a strong arts program, many of them have been in plays. I ask them if they learned their lines by rereading the script. Of course not, they learn by trying to recite them from memory. We talk about making and using higher quality flashcards as outlined on Pooja Agarwal's retrieval practice website, RetrievalPractice.org.

Recently, that study skills class and I stumbled upon a way to construct a practice test using modified flashcards. We talked for a while about how to think like a teacher to write a variety of questions. I gave them half an hour to write fifteen questions on the chapter they most needed to study. The question was on the front of the card as it would appear on a test. The answer was on the back. I realized halfway through that if they laid them out with the question side up, they would have a practice test. I had them trade places with someone and "take their test." Then, they flipped the cards over and checked their answers against what was now an answer key. We discussed the benefit of doing it this way at home rather than using flashcards traditionally or just writing questions on a list. The benefit we liked best was that it was manipulable. They could remove questions they had gotten right with high confidence. They could change the order by shuffling them. They could do it multiple times without getting bored. It could be for the entire chapter or just for the questions they most needed to retrieve again, and they could start making them on the first day of the chapter and keep adding to it each day until they had a full set of questions at the end of the chapter. There are many retrieval techniques, but we had a lot of fun with this one in addition to it being beneficial, so I'll be encouraging it in the future.

Be aware that many students will react negatively to retrieval practice, especially in the beginning. Don't let that stop you from using it. In the same way I hate it when Matt stops to watch us kickbox on our own because I'm afraid I will do something wrong, students don't like the feel of retrieval practice because they are afraid of appearing silly. This is why they tend to revert to rereading the chapter for study, in spite of its lack of effectiveness. It feels safer and more comfortable to run your eyes back over a page than it does to risk saying or writing the answer to a question with the potential to be incorrect. With middle and high school students, I find it helpful to explain my reasoning to them and make a big deal out of the benefits whenever I can to get them past that initial resistance. They may still not like it, but they will like its effects on their eventual confidence level and their grades. Don't throw them into the deep end all at once. Start slowly, perhaps with bellwork questions. Then add exit tickets or mid-class checks at another time. Once you start doing it, you will get a feel for when retrieval is needed and gain flexibility with it, but you should overcome your inertia by starting with one method that you can use every day.

In her book *What Every Teacher Needs to Know*, Jade Pearce summarizes the research on retrieval practice, encouraging teachers to

- use different formats;
- require that it be done from memory;
- make it adequately challenging while giving students a chance to be successful;
- include all types of thinking levels;
- scaffold where needed;
- employ it in a spaced and repeated way;
- involve all students simultaneously.

Retrieval practice isn't one thing. It is any way that you can get students to bring information back into their working memory. As you get more comfortable, feel free to be creative with it. Mix up techniques occasionally, focusing on the goal of retrieval rather than one method. This will keep students from getting bored, help them get past fear of wrong answers, and even provide them with multiple ways they can engage with it on their own while studying at home.

10 Formative Assessment

Twenty-one years ago, I taught an Algebra IB class, the second-half of an algebra course for those who need their algebra at a slower pace. I was new to the school, so I thought there had been a scheduling error. When I told my new administrator that I had no training or experience in teaching math, she said, "If you can teach physics, you can teach Algebra I." I'm still not certain that is true, but this was a small school that wanted me to fill a need, so I gave it a go. As I set about teaching students to graph quadratic functions, factor binomial expressions, and solve exponential growth problems, I taught them to follow steps the way one might follow a recipe. There were only eight students, and they were already the ones who needed algebra at a slower pace, so this felt like the right approach. Math teachers out there, please remember that I had no training or experience in math instruction and was just doing the best I could. I now know this isn't teaching them mathematical reasoning, but I didn't know how to do that.

During class, things seemed like they were going well. Then, I gave a test. Things were NOT going well. One student could do the first step of a problem before getting lost while others didn't even know how to begin. I was confused by the differences in their approaches, so I started analyzing my classroom practice and realized why there was a disconnect. When we solved problems together in class, we were solving them *together* as a group. It seemed like the best way to engage every student, but I didn't realize that this method was masking individual deficiencies in understanding. They could only solve problems as a group. Liz knew how to do step one, which gave Eric just enough momentum to do step two. Drew could do step three. I didn't have enough math experience to recognize that they were dependent on each other, so we all suffered from the illusion of competence until they had to do problems without help.

I realized that I needed to check in more frequently with each individual. I started giving exit tickets every day and a low-stakes quiz each Friday about what we had covered during the week. Once I started doing that, I had a better sense of where each student was in their competence with each skill. I would do more things to check for understanding in real time now, but these two things meant their test grades improved, and we all learned more. This was my first real-life lesson in formative assessment.

If you look for a definition of formative assessment, you will find a wide variety of thoughts. Kevin Washburn calls formative assessment "a teacher's assessment activities *while a student is learning*." Dylan William describes it as "any activity that provides information about student learning and enables teachers to adapt teaching to meet student needs." Both of these are true, one placing the emphasis on the timing while the other places the emphasis on the purpose. Since formative assessment covers a lot of thoughts, the best comprehensive definition I found is a little clunky. The Council of Chief State School Officers issued this definition: "Formative assessment is a planned, ongoing process used by all students and teachers during learning and teaching to elicit and use evidence of student learning to improve student understanding of intended disciplinary learning outcomes and support students to become self-directed learners." That's a lot of thoughts in one sentence, so let's break it down.

Formative assessment is planned. You do a lot of informal sizing up of your students at every moment of class. That constant stream of input has value. Teachers collect a lot of information just by remaining sensitive to our surroundings during class, looking at their faces for signs of confusion, listening for sounds of understanding, and feeling the general vibe of the room. In their book *Checking for Understanding*, Douglas Fisher and Nancy Frey acknowledge the ubiquitous nature of the data we collect just by maintaining awareness during a lesson. They say, "Talented educators know that the opportunities for fine-grained analysis of student learning are all around us. Each time we host a discussion with students, examine a child's writing, or listen closely to a question, there's a chance to assess formatively."

But, the informal process isn't enough. It's easy to misread the vibe in the room and allow ourselves to believe that, because it feels like the class understands, every member of the class does too. Real formative assessment is planned ahead of time to gain information about what students have learned and should be carefully thought through while planning lessons. What data do you need? It depends on the lesson, but you know what the essentials are, so plan questions for them. Ask yourself, "What do I most need to know if they understand before I move on with the lesson?"

Second, formative assessment is ongoing. When I was in college, I took a physical chemistry course. Occasionally, the professor would ask if anyone had questions. He was a sweet man, but like a lot of high-level science professors, he was not adept at reading social cues. The deer in the headlights expressions on the faces of his students might have clued him in that we were all lost, but if no one answered when he asked if we had questions, he assumed we were all fine and moved on with his lecture. One day, I said, "Dr. Collins, I would have to understand more than I do in order to even form a question." If he had been asking us questions rather than requesting ours, he would have had a better idea of whether or not his lesson was being absorbed.

During my first years of teaching, I fell into the same trap, thinking I was getting enough information by simply asking, "Does everyone understand?" I had been the type of student who would have said, "No, actually I don't. Can you repeat that? Here's what questions I still have." I didn't know that most students weren't like that, so when I asked if there were any questions, I wrongly assumed that the lack of questions meant everyone was on track. While we can get a lot of information from the informal and unplanned moments, we aren't all going to be equally good at interpreting that data, leading to wrong conclusions. We need something planned, ongoing, and specific. If I have preplanned moments throughout the lesson to stop and check for student understanding, I will be much more effective at gathering and interpreting valuable information. These moments become easier to plan with experience because you know where the sticking points were in previous years and what the essentials are in each lesson.

It is crucial that formative assessment be used by all those involved in the learning process. I once heard someone say, "The biggest problem with communication is the illusion that it is happening." The same can be said of learning. If students don't know they are confused, they won't ask questions, and even when they know they are lost, they often don't know what questions to ask. If I don't know they have misconceptions, I won't correct them. Formative assessment should provide data for the teacher to reflect on and use to improve their teaching, either in the moment or at the beginning of the next lesson. By getting a glimpse into the minds of our students as they learn, we can adjust learning activities, change pace, reteach with refined explanations, or provide more practice. Otherwise, I might as well be a video recording.

Additionally, formative assessments are a way to keep students motivated throughout the entire teaching process. If your students are like mine, they have gotten the idea that they can check out during class and learn material later from other sources. I don't know why they want to teach themselves in their free time, but it is something I've noticed in recent years and especially after our return from the pandemic lockdowns. Frequent formative assessment, whether in the form of white retrieval questions, in class practice problems, or review games, requires them to stay engaged because they know there will soon be a check of their understanding. It helps us to know where they are, and it motivates them to remain engaged and working. In his book *Uprise*, Kevin Washburn states that "making yourself aware of progress nourishes motivation."

Washburn also discusses the value of practice and feedback, saying, "Mastery, where we can perform a skill without thinking, takes time to develop. First, we establish accuracy, then we build efficiency. That's why patience is a critical component of the learning mindset. First attempts require feedback and adjustment before additional tries increase accuracy." There are neurological underpinnings for this practice. In their book *Uncommon Sense Teaching*, Barbara Oakley, Beth Rogowsky, and Terrence Sejnowski make the point that frequent formative assessments "encourage the creation of solid links in the neocortex, so the student doesn't have to depend on the not-very-long-lasting indexing links of the hippocampus." Put more simply, frequent formative assessments produce myelination, firmly planting information in long-term memory.

By the way, you can also plan your adaptation. Dylan William advocates for planning your reteaching based on the likely incorrect answers you get during formative assessments, calling it "building plan B into plan A." The more experience you get teaching the same content, the better you will become at predicting the wrong answers students might give, and you can predict the misconceptions that cause them. He describes these carefully planned points of formative assessment as hinge questions. "By planning at least a few questions carefully, teachers can get better-quality evidence about what their students can and can't do in time to do something about it."

So what are the best ways to engage in formative assessment? In his 2011 article "Formative Assessment: A Critical Review," Randy Elliott Bennett concludes that "the term, 'formative assessment', does not yet represent a well-defined set of artifacts or practices." Over a decade later, much work has been done, but we still do not have a tried and true list of ways to assure high-quality assessment. It is universally agreed that questioning students is a good way to gain insight into their learning, but not all questioning is equally effective. John Hattie places its effect size at up to 0.46, which makes it highly effective, but he also acknowledges that "the effects of questioning vary mainly due to the types of questions asked." All methods from quick retrieval in class to practice test questions to homework vary in efficacy, depending on the quality of the question as well as the feedback given.

Does that leave us lost? Should we give up on formative assessment simply because the effectiveness of techniques is hard to measure. Of course not. Research matters, but it's not the only thing that matters. Teaching is both a science and an art. Books like Craig Barton's *Tips for Teachers* and websites like RetrievalPractice.org provide resources and suggestions for improving our checks for understanding.

We can assess ourselves as we assess students, making note of what techniques provided us with valuable information and what techniques were a waste of time. We can discuss ideas with other teachers about what formative assessment methods have worked for them. Who is the most effective teacher in your school? Ask what he or she does to check for understanding. I asked the most effective teachers I could find and included their suggestions in the following pages.

Good teaching requires a lot of reflection. Remaining vigilant in the classroom allows us to collect data about student learning. Taking some time after class to reflect on that information allows us to be responsive to the students in front of us rather than sticking solely to our plans. While that may require leaving out something you intended to teach, when there is a choice between covering all of our curriculum and having students learn well, we should always come down on the side of having students learn well. Otherwise we will have wasted our time covering more.

Formative Assessment Techniques

(Definitely NOT a complete list - add your own!)

Entrance Tickets and Exit Tickets
Cold Calling
Full Class Response with Mini-Whiteboards
Full Class Digital Response (Socrative, Slido, Padlet, etc.)
Guided Practice of Skills
Choral Response
Turn and Talk
Short Review Games
Low or No Stakes Quizzes

Figure 10.1 Formative assessment techniques.

Formative assessment comes in a number of forms. The majority of mine comes from the GoFormative bellwork assignments and whiteboard retrieval opportunities I described in Chapter 9. That gives me enough real-time information that I don't feel the need to have a weekly quiz that requires grading. I'm not criticizing that; I found weekly quizzes more than a little helpful in the math class I described earlier because I didn't have enough math experience to assess their learning on the fly. Zane Smitley uses occasional quizzes to firm up information in AP biology before he presents them with the challenge of using those skills in more complex ways. He also pays close attention to their activity during his whiteboard retrieval activities. While he allows them to use their notes if they really need to, he looks at how often they need them, especially if it is a question he has asked more than once. If they are relying heavily on their notes, he knows he probably needs to reteach some aspect of the content.

The quickest form of assessment has been described in numerous books and conference workshops, having students assess their own understanding on a scale of one to five and hold up that number of fingers. I use this method sparingly, but I have a couple of caveats. I mentioned earlier that students do not usually have an accurate assessment of their own understanding, so I would never make this my only form of data collection. I'm really looking more at their confidence level than their level of understanding. You may remember that the definition of formative assessment at the beginning of this chapter described it as a method for both teachers and students. I had an interesting conversation with a fellow teacher on Twitter about this. He said, "I don't know what to do with the feedback I get from this method. If half the class is at 1 or 2 and the other half is at 3 or 4, how am I supposed to adapt? Do I re-teach it or not?" I replied that those numbers don't change my plans. I use it more for them than for me. I have them hold up their fingers after the first or second example we have done in class. I don't expect many high numbers because I do it early in the process. No matter what the group of numbers, I already have planned to do another example or two. Those at a higher level might work those examples more quickly while the ones with lower numbers may still rely on me for the next step, but they will all engage in the next examples. I then ask them to hold their fingers up again. Usually, the lower numbers have climbed by at least one level, so I remind them that practicing improves their abilities. If the ones that initially rated themselves a bit higher haven't climbed, I ask them if they were a bit overconfident after the first examples, and we talk about ways to better judge our own understanding rather than assume we pick up everything quickly. Like I said, this method is more for them than it is for me.

Formative assessment should inform my next step in teaching. In my indoor cycle classes at the YMCA, all of the instructors are paying attention, but one of them, Tom, engages in high-level formative assessment. Tom gets off of his bike and walks around to look at the screens. Am I on the tension level he said we should be? Have I achieved the distance he's looking for? Sometimes, I have, and he is quick to congratulate me. Sometimes, I can't do what he asked me to do that day. He looks at what I am doing and asks for a little more even if it isn't his original goal. He really wants me to reach a mile in three minutes, but it has only happened one time, so he looks at where I was on my last lap and adjusts his goal for me. If I achieved 0.85 miles on my previous lap, he asks me to push for 0.9 miles on this one. He adapts his expectations based on my current performance, but he doesn't lower the bar to the level of my current performance because he wants me to grow. He uses the data to adjust his "lesson plan" to a place that is possible for me but still challenging.

Finding the sweet spot of challenging but doable is what formative assessment is for. When I circulate my classroom and see that students are not where I planned for them to be, it is not the time to hand out independent practice. It may be time to adjust, saying, "You know that homework I had posted? I'm not sure we are ready for that. Why don't we do those problems together in class tomorrow?" This allows for diffuse mode and sleep to create stronger links that we can use when we practice again.

When describing her formative assessment methods, Hannah Eichhorst told me, "I just try to keep them talking to me about their learning." She sometimes asks questions to individuals in cold calls. Other times, she asks for volunteers. She has class discussions in which everyone is expected to contribute something. The combination of all these "talk to me about your learning" scenarios gives her valuable information about what needs to be explained again or if she needs to pull a few students in for reteaching during their study hall. Holly Kane, a sixth-grade teacher, asks her students to pretend they are going to teach the content to someone a year younger than they are. She has them prepare a slide presentation with the relevant information and write what they would say if they were explaining it to a younger student. She said, "When students have to rephrase new information and are asked to write, draw, or diagram it in a way that make sense to them they are better able to recall the content later," making this method not only an act of formative assessment but also rich encoding and retrieval.

My friend Dru Murphy teaches transitional kindergarten. She spends most of the day engaged in formative assessment. As they learn new things, she continuously circles back to what they have already learned, asking them questions about the building blocks as they build the concept. Most of her students enthusiastically throw their hands up with every question, and she makes sure to call on every student. She sometimes has them say their answers in unison, in the form of a chant or a song, or come and point to the right answer on a chart in her classroom. What she does requires a lot of energy, and I am in awe when I watch her; but all of this questioning and answering is giving her valuable information about where her students are and whether she needs to revisit a concept after lunch or the following day.

When it comes to skills, there is no better way to engage in formative assessment than to set them off on a practice example and circulate. A quick look over their shoulder will reveal if they are able to work independently, need some prompting to get past a sticking point, or don't even know how to start. If a large number of students don't know where to start, stop everything and reteach. If a lot of them seem to be stuck at the same point or you have answered the same question for more than two students, it may be wise to pause the work and re-explain just that one part. Letting them struggle through something they aren't ready for isn't going to help them. Productive struggle is only valuable if it produces results; otherwise, it is just struggle.

Marcia Wingerd, the media specialist at my school, is available to teach media literacy skills in our seventh- through twelfth-grade classrooms. One of the things she teaches is the citation of images. After explicitly teaching the format and the tools needed for proper citation, she asks them to find an image they might use in a project and has them create a citation for that image. They insert both into a Padlet, so she is able to tell from their products whether they have absorbed the necessary information about that skill. If several are missing an important piece of the citation, she knows that she should reteach that part of the process.

Donna Howard, a high school English teacher, told me she is less concerned with the method of formative assessment than the timing. She breaks the instruction down into smaller chunks and assesses learning between them. This is a wise use of the exit ticket during the lesson. Exit tickets are a common practice of formative assessment, but if you wait to do them at the end of class as their name implies, it can be harder to adapt. Don't let the name limit your use of this excellent technique. You can make it a mid-lesson ticket and adapt immediately. Just say, "You know what? I need to know if you can do this on your own before we move on. Do this problem, and put the answer on Socrative." You'll see the incoming answers in real time and get a quick sense of where the class is. "Okay, guys, you all seem ready to move on" or "Well, I think we need to do another example together" is great when you still have fifteen minutes of class time left to accomplish either of those things, but it is less effective when they are on their way out of the door.

The timing can be varied, depending on what you are trying to assess. I frequently ask Marcia to come into my classroom to teach about research, citations, or 3D print software. She begins the lesson with a few questions in Slido to gauge their prior understanding of the material she is about to teach. About halfway through, she may ask them to answer a few questions as retrieval of what she has just told them. It's a check for understanding and also a way to engage those who may have drifted, but it also allows her to adjust her teaching if they haven't quite grasped the concept. At the end, she asks a question or two that will help her to verify that they have learned what she was teaching. Because she uses a platform where all students answer, she knows that she is assessing all of their learning, not just the learning of a confident volunteer. She is getting an accurate measure of the entire group.

Cassidy Scholten's elementary class periods are too short to allow for much adaptation during class. She uses think-pair-share and listens carefully to their conversations in case she needs to jump quickly on a misconception, but her primary use of formative assessment is a "trivia game" at the end of the period. Her third-grade classes have to line up at the lab door to walk back to their regular classroom together, so she asks each table a formative assessment question. When they get one correct, they are dismissed to stand in line at the door. This tells her what to revisit the next time they meet. In her sixth-grade classes, they have exit tickets on Google Forms, which gives her enough feedback to know how to start the next class as well and often repeats the question as a warm-up to take advantage of spaced retrieval.

In his book *Tips for Teachers*, Craig Barton gives ten ideas to consider when using exit tickets. I won't take the space to discuss all ten here, but he has some thoughts I found quite valuable. First, exit tickets should be quick to ask because it is a check for understanding, not a quiz. Second, they should include questions everyone could get right if they learned what you had hoped they would in the lesson. It isn't a good time for the extra challenging question because you are trying to assess whether they learned the expected skill or content. Third, the exit ticket should deliver useful data about what misconceptions they may have. When crafting a multiple choice question, each wrong answer should be based on a common misconception. That way, you know where they are going wrong. On his *Tips for Teachers* podcast, he said, "When checking for understanding, the question matters a lot. If they can get the answer right with incorrect thinking, you haven't actually checked for understanding." This level of quality in exit ticket creation requires careful planning, so don't feel pressured to have one for every lesson right away. If there is content that created friction in the past, start there.

When thinking about the variety and depth of your formative assessments, consider ways you might involve more than recall questions. Melanie Dunning, for example, checks her chemistry students' understanding of molarity by taking them into the lab and having them make a solution at a specified concentration. They have to write down their process so she can check the concentration of the solution they have made. Zane Smitley's use of flawed graphs, as described in Chapter 8, requires analytical thinking in addition to recall.

My friend Nathan Dewey teaches Bible and history. He engages in many types of formative assessment, but what stuck with me was what he told me about questions where students must articulate their learning in writing. He said, "free response assessments reveal how imprecise his students' understanding is." They may be able to use the correct vocabulary, but if they are using it in ways that don't quite fit the core concept he is teaching, he knows that he needs to ask more questions later to help them put their fledgling knowledge into deeper use.

While we mostly think of it as a way to find deficiencies in learning, formative assessment has the potential to increase student confidence about their learning as well. They can see what they are getting right. For one week of most summers, I have been the photographer at a camp called Royal Family Kids Camp. There is a VBS (Vacation Bible School) style session every day, where kids sing, listen to stories, see plays, and have an object lesson—all around the big idea for the day. The woman who teaches these lessons is a retired middle school teacher, so she knows the value of formative assessment and student engagement. She asks the campers, "What's today's big idea?" and "What was yesterday's big idea?" throughout the week. She asks for examples from the stories and asks them about the theme verse they are memorizing for the week. When she calls on a camper, and they get the answer right, you can see the pride in their faces. They leave that room feeling like they have learned something important, and they have. Not only that, they have had the chance to publicly demonstrate it. The same is true in our classrooms. Imagine if every student could feel like they had the chance to get something right every day in your classroom. That is possible through well-crafted formative assessment.

Let's talk about grading for a second. You do not have to grade every assessment, and this is especially true of formative assessments. They are meant to size up a group or individual's understanding quickly, so you can adapt your teaching. Once they have accomplished that goal, you don't need them anymore. Don't feel bad about dropping them in the trash after they have served their purpose. I'm a big believer in the value of putting things on paper, but if paper makes you feel like you must grade it, use something else. Closing the Socrative window will feel less like you are neglecting something than dropping papers in the trash will. It's in our psychology from years of teacher training to think everything must be graded, but you should do a lot more formative assessments than you are prepared to (or even able to) grade. You'll avoid the sense of guilt by planning your formative assessments in a way that cannot be graded, like a whiteboard that gets erased soon after you look at the answers.

Engaging in formative assessment will change the way you view teaching and learning. You will recognize that misconceptions affect learning if they are not addressed quickly. You will find that students didn't ask questions because they didn't know they were confused until you dug a little deeper into their understanding. You will proceed to the next part of the lesson with more confidence that students have the foundation they need for it rather than hoping they will catch up later. If you aren't concerned with grading it, it won't be scary to students and will simply become part of your classroom culture.

Conclusion

Teachers, your task is difficult. It may, in fact, be impossible, which is why it is important that you don't try to do it alone. You walk into a classroom every day, expected to equip, challenge, and inspire every student, regardless of background, home support, past educational experience, or interest level in your subject. You may or may not have the support of your administration when it comes to classroom disruptions. You likely don't have the budget you need to properly carry out the things you would like to do, so you employ your creative skills to work around lack of supplies. During the pandemic, many people found out how difficult it was to teach their own children at home and went online to praise you, but the whiplash was strong when they changed their minds a few months later, expecting you to have figured it out by the fall. As with all of the other issues in our society, education has become polarized along political lines, and you are in the middle, just trying to do your job. And you do it. You do it well, and you keep trying to improve by talking to colleagues about your practice and reading books like this one.

Every day, you equip your students with the information they need to be good decision-makers. This is no small task, and the culture in which we exist wants to add to the curriculum, making you the solution to all of society's problems while simultaneously blaming you for being the source of those same ills. It only takes a few days on social media for you to see a post about the life skills someone believes schools should be teaching, from sewing on buttons to filling out tax forms to car repair. Others push for college level courses to be included in high school, wanting every student to have an associate's degree by the time they graduate. They want you to include all the things they learned in school and become incensed if you remove something like cursive writing from the curriculum, but they also want their child to be prepared for the future, so it is important that you teach technology skills. Of course, no one wants to add minutes to the day or days to the school year, so you are expected to teach all of this between 8:00 a.m. and 3:00 p.m. and not give any homework so children have time to play after they get home from soccer practice. The mere act of equipping them is Herculean, and it is the most basic level of your job.

You are also meant to challenge students at all levels of the ability spectrum. In the same classroom, you have a child with profound learning disabilities and those with intelligence higher than your own and the full range of academic levels in between. You have students who may have had a bad experience with science or math in the past and enter your classroom skittish while others suggest lab experiments to you because they spend their free time reading about them online. Finding the appropriate level of challenge for students who have experienced some trauma with math is difficult, especially since you have a few students in the same classroom who are thrilled by math and want more challenging problems to solve than you are prepared to teach. (Yes, that child does exist; his name is Jacob, and I taught him chemistry and physics.) You ask ALL of them to perform better than they believe they are able to at things they don't think they are good at. You are supposed to be fun and joyful and engaging while you demand more from a child than that child (and sometimes their parent) thinks you should be asking for. You don't always find the right level, but you are always trying.

The best of you inspire, asking your students to look beyond the grade, the curriculum, and the tests to see what they can do with their education. While I loved learning in all of my school subjects, history was my least favorite. Yet, I had a middle school history teacher named Mr. Watkins whose passion for the story of Czar Nicholas and Alexandra of Russia was so strong that I couldn't help but be drawn into it. A decade later, I found myself in an art museum with tears streaming down my face as I stood in front of Alexandra's crown and a desk used by Nicholas. I don't normally have emotional responses to furniture and jewelry, but a teacher inspired me in a way that made me care (and had nothing to do with using that knowledge or getting a job). You have a student who "doesn't like science" on the first day they enter your classroom who will tell stories someday about the teacher who made them care about why they couldn't mix bleach with ammonia or understand why they felt lighter when going to lower floors in a fast elevator. Some may go into medicine because you taught them anatomy, but most will simply have a better understanding of their own body and how it works and be enriched by that. You build up students into people with a broader view of the world than they would have if you hadn't been their teacher. It's an awesome thing to consider.

And that, friends, is just the academic part of your job; I have not included all of the social counseling, emotional baggage, and safety concerns you keep in balance. You know which students shouldn't be put in a group together and who needs a friend to sit with at lunch. You are the frontline of reporting abuse and the shoulder to cry on for many students and colleagues. You make hundreds of decisions per day, often without time to reflect on them thoroughly. Are you starting to understand why you are so tired at the end of each day?

The science of learning principles described in this book are not meant to add another thing to your already overflowing plate. Using them should, in the long run, make things easier for you because you will be working with the students' brains in the way they learn best. In his article "Evidence Informed Wisdom," Tom Sherrington reminds us:

> Research isn't telling us what to do. It can't. However, it can inform our decisions. Teachers have wisdom in bucket loads—from their experience of previous scenarios accumulated over time; from their interactions with the specific students they are teaching now; from their engagement with the curriculum and its modes of assessment. Into that mix comes some ideas derived from studies into learning, memory, observed classroom practices … and that all has to be filtered, assimilated and woven into the fabric of our understanding of what we should do in order to secure our students' learning and the things they and we need to do today and tomorrow.

The longer you teach, the more fluid you become at incorporating all of this into your decision-making.

In her book *The Extended Mind*, Annie Murphy Paul says, "Instead of heedlessly driving the brain like a machine, we will think more intelligently when we treat it as the context-sensitive organ it is." You know your context better than anyone else, so combining your wisdom with evidence-based principles should eventually cut down on remediation and tutoring sessions, freeing up time for you to design genuinely impactful lessons that are right for you and your students, not force you into a cookie cutter set of practices. As Stanislas Dehaene says in *How We Learn*, "Genuine pedagogical creativity can only come from full awareness of the range of available strategies and the ability to choose carefully from them, with full knowledge of their impact on students." The research is giving you a framework in which to think, but you must still use your professional judgment to decide what is best in your own classroom.

The work you do matters. It matters every day. You owe it to yourself and your students to use the best techniques you can. I hope the ideas you found in this book will be helpful and reduce your stress load rather than add to it. I hope it gives you more confidence in the umpteen thousand decisions you have to make in your career. Be encouraged that just by reaching out to find good information, you have taken the first step to improving the way you serve the students in front of you. Share it with other teachers. Share it with students and their parents. Showing your work shows your wisdom.

Then, get some well-earned rest.

Bibliography

Abdul, P. (1991). "Vibeology" [Song]. On *Spellbound*. Virgin.

Agarwal, P. K. (2019, November 18). "Make Flashcards More Powerful with These 3 Tips—Retrieval Practice." *Retrieval Practice*. https://www.retrievalpractice.org/strategies/2019/11/18/flashcards.

Agarwal, P. K., & Bain, P. M. (2019). *Powerful Teaching: Unleash the Science of Learning*. Wiley.

Al-Khalili, J., & Homan, R. (2010). "The Order of the Elements." *Chemistry: A Volatile History*. BBC. https://www.youtube.com/watch?v=37Mrhf7Ifbl.

Almarode, J., & Vandas, K. (2018). *Clarity for Learning: Five Essential Practices That Empower Students and Teachers*. SAGE.

Barton, C. (2022, March 10). "Adam Boxer" [Audio Podcast Episode]. In *Tips for Teachers*. https://tipsforteachers.co.uk/adam-boxer/.

Barton, C. (2022, March 10). "Dylan Wiliam" [Audio Podcast Episode]. In *Tips for Teachers*. https://tipsforteachers.co.uk/dylan-wiliam/.

Barton, C. (2022, March 29). "Dylan William Tips for Teachers" [Audio Podcast Episode]. In *Tips for Teachers*. https://tipsforteachers.co.uk/dylan-wiliam/.

Barton, C. (2023). *Tips for Teachers: 400+ Ideas to Improve Your Teaching: Hodder Education Group*. John Catt Educational.

Barton, C. (2024, March 15). "Tom Sherrington" [Audio Podcast Episode]. In *Tips for Teachers*. https://tipsforteachers.co.uk/tom-sherrington/.

Bennett, R. E. (2011). "Formative Assessment: A Critical Review." *Assessment in Education: Principles, Policy & Practice*, *18*(1), 5–25. https://doi.org/10.1080/0969594X.2010.513678.

Bigelow, M. (2017, February). "Scaffolding Science Skills." *National Science Teachers Association*. https://www.nsta.org/blog/scaffolding-science-skills.

Bobek, E., & Tversky, B. (2016). "Creating Visual Explanations Improves Learning." *Cogn. Research*, *1*(27). https://doi.org/10.1186/s41235-016-0031-6.

Boblett, N. (2012). "Scaffolding: Defining the Metaphor." *TESOL and Applied Linguistics*, *12*(2), 1–16. https://www.researchgate.net/publication/299534682_Scaffolding_Defining_the_Metaphor.

Bunge, M. (1969). "Analogy, Simulation, Representation." *Revue Internationale de Philosophie*, *23*(87[1]), 16–33. http://www.jstor.org/stable/23940647.

Busch, B. (@BradleyKBusch). (2024, March 21). "But what is the mechanism at play here? A recent meta-analysis on this suggest two potential mechanisms. They found retrieval" [Post]. *X*. https://x.com/BradleyKBusch/status/1770732518175621518.

Chandler, P., & Sweller, J. (1992). "The Split-Attention Effect as a Factor in the Design of Instruction." *British Journal of Educational Psychology*, *62*(2), 233–46. https://bpspsychub.onlinelibrary.wiley.com/doi/10.1111/j.2044-8279.1992.tb01017.x.

Christen, W., & Murphy, T. (1991). "Increasing Comprehension by Activating Prior Knowledge." *ERIC Digest*. https://files.eric.ed.gov/fulltext/ED328885.pdf.

Christodoulou, D. (2024, April 28). "Your Digital Education Transformation Strategy." *No More Marking*. https://substack.nomoremarking.com/p/your-digital-education-transformation.

Church, R. B., Garber, P., & Rogalski, K. (2007, January). "The Role of Gesture in Memory and Social Communication." *Gesture*, *7*(2), 137–58. https://www.jbe-platform.com/content/journals/10.1075/gest.7.2.02bre.

Corbett, E. P. J. (1971, October). "The Theory and Practice of Imitation in Classical Rhetoric." *College Composition and Communication*, *22*(3), 243–50. https://www.jstor.org/stable/356450?origin=crossref.

Cowan, N. (2001, October 30). "The Magical Number 4 in Short-Term Memory: A Reconsideration of Mental Storage Capacity." *Behavioral and Brain Sciences*, *24*(1), 87–114. https://www.cambridge.org/core/journals/behavioral-and-brain-sciences/article/magical-number-4-in-shortterm-memory-a-reconsideration-of-mental-storage-capacity/44023F1147D4A1D44BDC0AD226838496#.

Dehaene, S. (2021). *How We Learn: The New Science of Education and the Brain*. Penguin Books.

Deng, F., Gluckstein, J. A., & Larsen, D. P. (2015, October 23). "Student-Directed Retrieval Practice Is a Predictor of Medical Licensing Examination Performance." *Perspectives on Medical Education*, *4*(6), 308–13. https://pmejournal.org/articles/10.1007/S40037-015-0220-X.

Deng, Z. (2022). "Powerful Knowledge, Educational Potential and Knowledge-Rich Curriculum: Pushing the Boundaries." *Journal of Curriculum Studies*, *54*(5), 599–617. https://doi.org/10.1080/00220272.2022.2089538.

DeWitt, T. (2012, November). "Hey Science Teachers—Make It Fun." TED [Video]. YouTube. https://www.ted.com/talks/tyler_dewitt_hey_science_teachers_make_it_fun.

Duit, R. (1991). "The Role of Analogies and Metaphors in Learning Science." *Science Education*, *75*, 649–72. 10.1002/sce.3730750606.

Fields, R. (2015). "A New Mechanism of Nervous System Plasticity: Activity-Dependent Myelination." *Nature Reviews Neuroscience, 16*, 756–67. https://www.nature.com/articles/nrn4023#citeas.

Fisher, A. V., Godwin, K. E., & Seltman, H. (2014). "Visual Environment, Attention Allocation, and Learning in Young Children: When Too Much of a Good Thing May Be Bad." *Psychological Science, 25*(7), 1362–70. https://doi.org/10.1177/0956797614533801.

Fisher, D., & Frey, N. (2014). *Checking for Understanding: Formative Assessment Techniques for Your Classroom*. ASCD.

Fisher, D., Frey, N., & Hite, S. A. (2016). *Intentional and Targeted Teaching: A Framework for Teacher Growth and Leadership*. ASCD.

Grissmer, D., White, T., Buddin, R., Berends, M., Willingham, D., DeCoster, J., Duran, C., Helleman, C., Murrah, W., & Evans, T. (2023, July). "A Kindergarten Lottery Evaluation of Core Knowledge Charter Schools: Should Building General Knowledge Have a Central Role in Educational and Social Science Research and Policy?" *EdWorking Papers*. https://edworkingpapers.com/ai23-755.

Hanley, M., Khairat, M., Taylor, K., Wilson, R., Cole-Fletcher, R., & Riby, D. M. (2017). "Classroom Displays—Attraction or Distraction? Evidence of Impact on Attention and Learning from Children with and Without Autism." *Developmental Psychology, 53*(7), 1265–75. https://doi.org/10.1037/dev0000271.

Harris, P. (2015). "What Children Learn from Questioning." *ASCD, 73*(1). https://www.ascd.org/el/articles/what-children-learn-from-questioning.

Hattie, J. (n.d.). "Hattie Effect Size List—256 Influences Related to Achievement." *Visible Learning*. https://visible-learning.org/hattie-ranking-influences-effect-sizes-learning-achievement/.

Hattie, J., & Timperley, H. (2007). "The Power of Feedback." *Review of Educational Research, 77*(1), 81–112. https://doi.org/10.3102/003465430298487.

Heal, J. (2023, November 18). *Mental Models: How Cognitive Science Can Transform the Way You Learn and Teach* [Presentation], Learning and the Brain Fall Conference, Boston, MA, United States.

Hendrick, C. (2025, June 14). "The Most Important Memory Is Still the One Inside Your Head." *The Learning Dispatch*. https://carlhendrick.substack.com/p/the-most-important-memory-is-still.

Hoque, E. (2018, February). "Memorization: A Proven Method of Learning." *International Journal of Applied Research, 22*(III), 142–50. https://www.researchgate.net/publication/330825027_Memorization_A_Proven_Method_of_Learning.

Kalyuga, S., Chandler, P., & Sweller, J. (1999). "Managing Split-Attention and Redundancy in Multimedia Instruction." *Applied Cognitive Psychology, 13*(4), 351–71. https://doi.org/10.1002/(SICI)1099-0720(199908)13:4<351::AID-ACP589>3.0.CO;2-6.

Kasai, H., Fukuda, M., Watanabe, S., Hayashi-Takagi, A., & Noguchi, J. (2010). "Structural Dynamics of Dendritic Spines in Memory and Cognition." *Trends in Neurosciences*, *33*(3), 121–9. https://doi.org/10.1016/j.tins.2010.01.001.

Kirschner, P. A., & Hendrick, C. (2024). *How Learning Happens: Seminal Works in Educational Psychology and What They Mean in Practice*. Routledge.

Kirschner, P. A., Clark, R. E., & Sweller, J. (2012, January). "Putting Students on the Path to Learning: The Case for Fully Guided Instruction." *Research Gate*. https://www.researchgate.net/publication/281609208_Putting_students_on_the_path_to_learning_The_case_for_fully_guided_instruction.

Kirschner, P. A., Sweller, J., & Clark, R. E. (2006). "Why Minimal Guidance During Instruction Does Not Work: An Analysis of the Failure of Constructivist, Discovery, Problem-Based, Experiential, and Inquiry-Based Teaching." *Educational Psychologist*, *41*(2), 75–86. https://doi.org/10.1207/s15326985ep4102_1.

Klencklen, G., Lavenex, P. B., Brandner, C., & Lavenex, P. (2017, February). "Working Memory Decline in Normal Aging: Is It Really Worse in Space than in Color?" *Learning and Motivation*, *57*, 48–60. https://www.sciencedirect.com/science/article/abs/pii/S0023969017300127.

Kraft, U. (2005, April 1). "Unleashing Creativity." *Scientific American*. https://www.scientificamerican.com/article/unleashing-creativity/.

Lechuga, M. T., Ortega-Tudela, J. M., & Gómez-Ariza, C. J. (2024, March 13). "Retrieval-Based Concept Mapping Makes a Difference as a Retrieval Practice Activity: A Study with High School Students." *Frontiers in Education*, *9*. https://www.frontiersin.org/journals/education/articles/10.3389/feduc.2024.1287744/full.

Lemov, D. (@Doug_Lemov). (2024, January 2). "In the classroom, the implications of working memory and its limits are at least as important for teachers as they" [Post]. *X*. https://x.com/Doug_Lemov/status/1742191384847687795.

Lewis, C. S. (2001). *The Great Divorce*. HarperCollins.

Lyle, K. B., & Crawford, N. A. (2011). "Retrieving Essential Material at the End of Lectures Improves Performance on Statistics Exams." *Teaching of Psychology*, *38*(2), 94–7. https://doi.org/10.1177/0098628311401587.

Mccrea, P. (2024, March 14). "Re: The Power of Routines." Evidence Snacks email newsletter. Received by Beth Hawks, 14 March 2024.

Mccrea, P. (2024, March 21) "Re: Banking Routines." Evidence Snacks email newsletter. Received by Beth Hawks, 21 March 2024.

McDermott, K. B. & Roediger, H. L. (2024). "Memory (Encoding, Storage, Retrieval)." In R. Biswas-Diener & E. Diener (Eds.), *Noba Textbook Series: Psychology*. Champaign, IL: DEF. Retrieved from http://noba.to/bdc4uger.

Metz, N. (2014, June 21). "How to Memorize Lines: Tips from Top Chicago Stage Actors." *Chicago Tribune*. https://www.chicagotribune.com/2014/06/21/how-to-memorize-lines-tips-from-top-chicago-stage-actors/.

Noguchi, J., Haruo, K., Fukuda, M., Watanabe, S., & Hayashi-Takagi, A. (2010, March). "Structural Dynamics of Dendritic Spines in Memory and Cognition." *PubMed, 33*(3), 121–9. https://pubmed.ncbi.nlm.nih.gov/20138375/.

Norman, K. A., & O'Reilly, R. C. (2002, August 29). "Modeling Hippocampal and Neocortical Contributions to Recognition Memory: A Complementary Learning Systems Approach." *Psychological Review*. https://www.princeton.edu/~compmem/psyrev_inpress.pdf.

North Carolina Essential Standards—Physics. https://center.ncsu.edu/standards/NCES/Physics/. Accessed May 16, 2024.

NWEA. (2016). "4 Formative Assessment Practices That Make a Difference in Classrooms." *Northwest Evaluation Association*. https://files.eric.ed.gov/fulltext/ED567811.pdf.

Oakley, B. A. (2014). *A Mind for Numbers: How to Excel at Math and Science (Even If You Flunked Algebra)*. Penguin.

Oakley, B. A. (2019, November 18). *Digging Deeper into the Science of Learning* [Concurrent Session]. Learning and the Brain Fall Conference, Boston, MA, United States.

Oakley, B. A. (2023, November 18). *The Science of Learning: Building Memories and Effective Learners* [Keynote Address]. Learning and the Brain Fall Conference, Boston, MA, United States.

Oakley, B. A., Rogowsky, B., & Sejnowski, T. J. (2021). *Uncommon Sense Teaching: Practical Insights in Brain Science to Help Students Learn*. Penguin.

Oakley, B. A., Sejnowski, T. J., & McConville, A. (2018). *Learning How to Learn: How to Succeed in School Without Spending All Your Time Studying; A Guide for Kids and Teens*. Penguin.

Oxford Reference. (n.d.). "Discovery Learning." OxfordReference.com. https://www.oxfordreference.com/display/10.1093/oi/authority.20110803095721422.

Paas, F., & van Merriënboer, J. J. G. (2020). "Cognitive-Load Theory: Methods to Manage Working Memory Load in the Learning of Complex Tasks." *Current Directions in Psychological Science, 29*(4), 394–8. https://doi.org/10.1177/0963721420922183.

Palacio, J. (2024, June 2). *The Story of God*. Holy Trinity Anglican Church Evening Service [Sermon]. Raleigh, NC, United States.

Paul, A. M. (2021). *The Extended Mind: The Power of Thinking Outside the Brain*. Houghton Mifflin Harcourt.

Pearce, J. (2022). *What Every Teacher Needs to Know: How to Embed Evidence-Informed Teaching and Learning in Your School*. Bloomsbury Publishing.

Perry, T., Lea R., Jørgensen C. R., Cordingley P., Shapiro K., & Youdell D. (2021). *Cognitive Science Approaches in the Classroom: A Review of the Evidence*, Education Endowment Foundation. https://d2tic4wvo1iusb.cloudfront.net/production/

documents/guidance/Cognitive_science_approaches_in_the_classroom_-_A_review_of_the_evidence.pdf?v=1713514779.
Quintilian. (2015). *Institutes of Oratory, or, Education of an Orator*. Edited by C. Dozier & L. Honeycutt. Translated by J. S. Watson. Vol. Book X. CreateSpace.
Riches, A. (2020). *Teach Smarter: Efficient and Effective Strategies for Early Career Teachers*. Taylor & Francis Group.
Riches, A. (2022, June 29). "Modelling and Scaffolding in the Classroom Lessons Pedagogy Teaching Teachers." *SecEd*. https://www.sec-ed.co.uk/content/best-practice/modelling-and-scaffolding-in-the-classroom/.
Rodger, S., Murray, H. G., & Cummings, A. L. (2007). "Effects of Teacher Clarity and Student Anxiety on Student Outcomes." *Teaching in Higher Education*, *12*(1), 91–104. https://doi.org/10.1080/13562510601102255.
Roksa, J., Trolian, T. L., Blaich, C., & Wise K. (2017). "Facilitating Academic Performance in College: Understanding the Role of Clear and Organized Instruction." *Higher Education*, *74*, 283–300. https://doi.org/10.1007/s10734-016-0048-2.
Ruggerio, M. (2022, March 3). "Retrieve Note Taking." *Physics Teacher Momma*. https://physicsteachermomma.com/2022/03/03/retrieve-note-taking/.
Sherrington, T. (2021, July 19). "What Does It Mean to Be 'Evidence-Informed' in Teaching?" *Teacherhead*. https://teacherhead.com/2021/07/19/what-does-it-mean-to-be-evidence-informed-in-teaching/.
Singh, D., Norman, K. A., & Schapiro, A. C. (2022, October 24). "A Model of Autonomous Interactions Between Hippocampus and Neocortex Driving Sleep-Dependent Memory Consolidation." *PNAS*. https://www.pnas.org/doi/abs/10.1073/pnas.2123432119.
Tharby, A. (2019). *How to Explain Absolutely Anything to Absolutely Anyone: The Art and Science of Teacher Explanation*. Crown House.
The Holy Bible (English Standard Version). (2006). Crossway Bibles. Luke 6:40.
Trent, J. D. (2017). *For Sabbath's Sake: Embracing Your Need for Rest, Worship, and Community*. Upper Room Books.
Vredeveldt, A., Hitch, G. J., & Baddeley, A. D. (2011). "Eyeclosure Helps Memory by Reducing Cognitive Load and Enhancing Visualisation." *Memory & Cognition*, *39*, 1253–63. https://doi.org/10.3758/s13421-011-0098-8.
Washburn, K. D. (2010). *The Architecture of Learning: Designing Instruction for the Learning Brain*. Clerestory.
Washburn, K. D. (2012). *Thinking Is the Target* [Keynote Address]. ACSI Connexus Conference, Orlando, FL, United States.
Washburn, K. D. (2024). *Uprise: Building Resilience in Ourselves and Others*. Morgan James.
Watson, A. C. (2017). *Learning Begins: The Science of Working Memory and Attention for the Classroom Teacher*. Bloomsbury Academic.

Watson, E., & Busch, B. (2021). *The Science of Learning: 99 Studies That Every Teacher Needs to Know*. Routledge.

Weinberger, E. (2024) "Focused vs Diffuse Mode: Why Students Need Both." Staying Ahead of the Game. https://saotg.com/focused-vs-diffuse-mode-why-students-need-both/. Accessed June 17, 2024.

What Is Retrieval Practice? (2025). RetrievalPractice.org. Retrieved July 24, 2025, from https://www.retrievalpractice.org/why-it-works.

Widmayer, S. A. (2023) "Schema Theory: An Introduction." George Mason University.

Wilke R. R., & Straits, W. J. (2001, June 1). "The Effects of Discovery Learning in a Lower-division Biology Course." *Advances in Physiological Education*, *25*(2). https://journals.physiology.org/doi/full/10.1152/advances.2001.25.2.62#.

William, D. (2015, September). "Designing Great Hinge Questions." *Educational Leadership*, *73*(1), 40–4. https://eric.ed.gov/?id=EJ1075042.

Willingham, D. T. (2016, April 18). "On Metaphor, Memory, and John King." *Daniel Willingham Science and Education*. http://www.danielwillingham.com/daniel-willingham-science-and-education-blog/on-metaphor-memory-and-john-king.

Willingham, D. T. (2004, Summer). "The Privileged Status of Story." *American Educator*. https://www.aft.org/ae/summer2004/willingham.

Willingham, D. T. (2006, Spring). "How Knowledge Helps." *American Educator*. https://www.aft.org/ae/spring2006/willingham.

Willingham, D. T. (2009). *Why Don't Students Like School? A Cognitive Scientist Answers Questions About How the Mind Works and What It Means for the Classroom*. Wiley.

Willingham, D. T. (2023). *Outsmart Your Brain: Why Learning Is Hard and How You Can Make It Easy*. Gallery Books.

Wong, H. K., & Wong, R. T. (1991). *The First Days of School: How to Be an Effective Teacher*. Harry K. Wong.

Wright, C. M. (2018). "Revising the Definition of Formative Assessment." Council of Chief State School Officers. https://ccsso.org/sites/default/files/2018-06/Revising%20the%20Definition%20of%20Formative%20Assessment.pdf.

Zakrajsek, T. (2022). *The New Science of Learning: How to Learn in Harmony with Your Brain*. Stylus.

Index

About the Author

Beth Hawks is a learner, first, and a teacher, second. As such, she's an avid reader, committed church member, and passionate indoor cycle instructor. Powered by peanut butter and Diet Mt. Dew, she lives in Raleigh, NC, with her cat, Sherlock.

She taught middle and high school science for twenty-five years. After becoming enamored with the science of learning, she stepped out of the classroom and into consulting in 2024 and is now doing business as The Learning Hawk in order to spread her passion beyond her own school. She is still a substitute at the school she loves and works part-time at the YMCA of the Triangle that changed her middle-aged life.

Beth believes that life is best lived with a mix of curiosity and gratitude. You can find more of her thoughts on education and life on her blog at the website www.thelearninghawk.com.

www.ingramcontent.com/pod-product-compliance
Ingram Content Group UK Ltd.
Pitfield, Milton Keynes, MK11 3LW, UK
UKHW022004240826
474727UK00001B/7

9 798216 378501